eduqas

REVISE WJEC EDUQAS GCSE (9–1) IN English Language

REVISION GUIDE

Series Consultant: Harry Smith

Authors: Julie Hughes and David Grant

Reviewer: Esther Menon

Also available to support your revision:

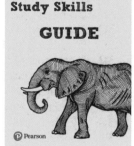

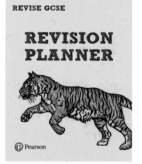

Contents

READING

WRITING

A small bit of small print
Eduqas publishes Sample Assessment Material and the Specification on its website. This is the official content and this book should be used in conjunction with it. The questions in *Now try this* have been written to help you practise every topic in the book. Remember: the real exam questions may not look like this.

Planning your exam time

Planning your exam time is extremely important. Running out of time is one of the most common ways that students lose marks in their exam. Plan your time to get the most out of every minute.

The paper

The **English Language GCSE** consists of two components, or exam papers. **Component 1** (20th Century Literature Reading and Creative Prose Writing) is worth 40% of your GCSE and **Component 2** (19th and 21st Century Non-fiction Reading and Transactional/Persuasive Writing) is worth 60%. Both components are split equally into **Reading** and **Writing**.

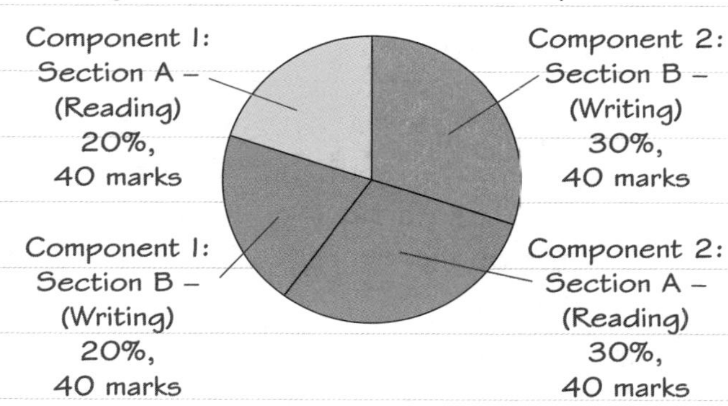

Also see pages 48–95 for more about writing

Component 1 exam is 1 hour 45 minutes long.
You should spend:

- 10 minutes reading the texts
- 50 minutes answering **Section A**
- 10 minutes planning **Section B**
- 35 minutes writing.

Component 2 exam is 2 hours long.
You should spend:

- 10 minutes reading the texts
- 50 minutes answering **Section A**
- 30 minutes on each of the two writing questions.

The first 10 minutes

Spend the first 10 minutes of each exam reading the texts and the questions you will be asked about them. For example:

1. **Read the questions**. What do you need to look for when you read the source texts?
2. **Skim read** the source texts to get a sense of the main ideas and themes.
3. **Read the texts carefully**, annotating them when you find information you will need in your answers.

How long to spend on a question?

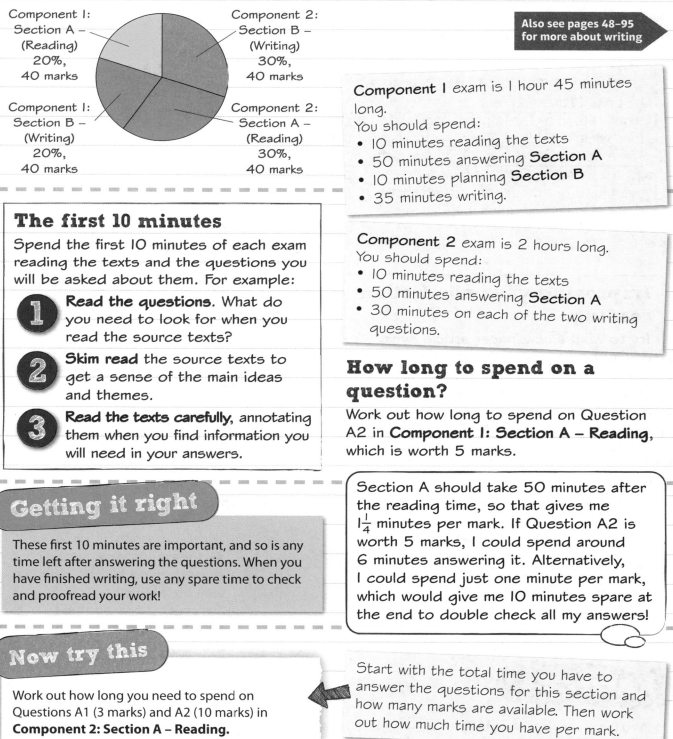

Work out how long to spend on Question A2 in **Component 1: Section A – Reading**, which is worth 5 marks.

Section A should take 50 minutes after the reading time, so that gives me $1\frac{1}{4}$ minutes per mark. If Question A2 is worth 5 marks, I could spend around 6 minutes answering it. Alternatively, I could spend just one minute per mark, which would give me 10 minutes spare at the end to double check all my answers!

Getting it right

These first 10 minutes are important, and so is any time left after answering the questions. When you have finished writing, use any spare time to check and proofread your work!

Now try this

Work out how long you need to spend on Questions A1 (3 marks) and A2 (10 marks) in **Component 2: Section A – Reading.**

Start with the total time you have to answer the questions for this section and how many marks are available. Then work out how much time you have per mark.

Reading texts explained

You will sit two papers for your exam: **Component 1** and **Component 2**. Each one has a **Reading** section (Section A) and a **Writing** section (Section B). You will meet different types of text in each.

Component 1: Section A – Reading

This will feature an extract from one work of **fiction** written in the **20th century**. The extract will be approximately 500–800 words, or around 60–100 lines in length. It could be from any literary genre.

Improving your fiction reading

Prepare by reading widely and independently outside lesson time, and make sure you are familiar with a variety of literary genres.

As you read, start to think about how and why the author has created **particular characters** and **atmospheres**.

Extract from Rebecca. *Full text on page 96. Lines 1–5.*

Last night I dreamt I went to Manderley again. It seemed to me I stood by the iron gate leading to the drive, and for a while I could not enter, for the way was barred to me. There was a padlock and a chain upon the gate. I called in my dream to the lodge-keeper, and had no answer, and peering closer through the rusted spokes of the gate I saw that the lodge was uninhabited.

- It is a dream, could be a nightmare?
- References to being locked out, suggests something frightening inside?
- Narrator is alone, could therefore be in danger?

Improving your non-fiction reading

Try to read a newspaper article every day, either in print form or online. Use your local or school library to access autobiographies and biographies. For 19th-century texts, use a search engine as there is a lot of material available free online.

Component 2: Section A – Reading

You will be given two **non-fiction** texts of about 900–1200 words in total. One will be from the **19th century**, the other from the **21st century**.

Non-fiction texts: e.g. letters; extracts from biographies/autobiographies, diaries, reports and articles; digital and multi-modal texts from newspapers, magazines and the internet

Start to think about the author's **purpose**, **tone** and **point of view**.

Extract from Who'd Be a Paper Boy? *Full text on page 100. Lines 25–31.*

You can have some sympathy for the kids. Standards in literacy and numeracy have fallen so steeply that it can be a real struggle identifying door names and numbers, and the Sunday papers are now so heavy that your averagely obese teenager just doesn't have the strength or stamina for the job.

- 'kids' rather than 'children' suggests informal article?
- Humour used to entertain as well as inform.
- Sarcastic tone suggests author's view is that children are lazy.

Now try this

Read the next two paragraphs (lines 34–44) of *Who'd Be a Paper Boy?* by John Crace on page 100. Note down your ideas about purpose, audience and the author's point of view.

Reading questions explained 1

You will need to answer certain **types of question** in the exam. The questions are based on extracts that you will not have seen before.

The skills you are tested on in these questions are called **assessment objectives**.

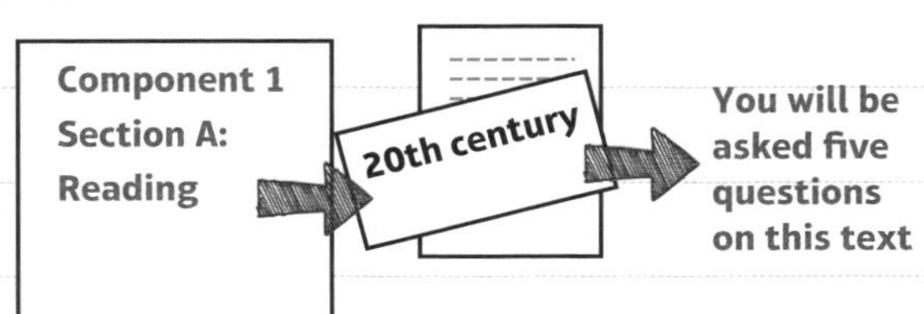

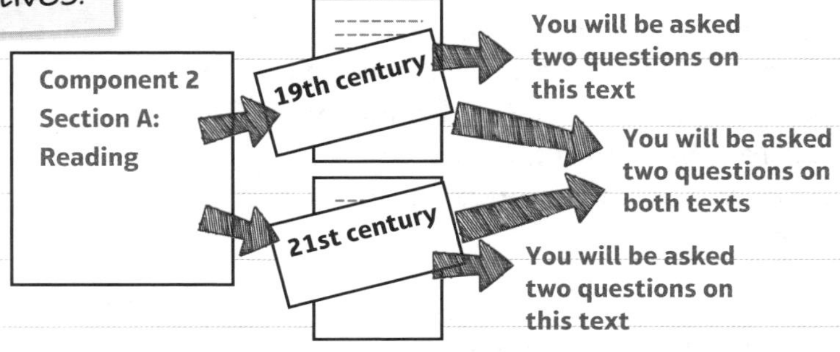

The questions on this page are sample questions and do not need to be answered.

Assessment objective 1

Assessment objective 1 tests your ability to **identify and explain** the information in a text.

Questions beginning 'A' appear in Section A, Reading.

These are examples of the types of question that will be used to test this skill.

A1 List **five** actions taken by the passengers before the boat tipped. **(5 marks)**

A3 (a) What does the writer mean by 'I have had some rankles in my lifetime'? **(1 mark)**

To revise these question types, see pages 10–11

To answer the following question you will need to use both texts.

A5 According to both writers, what are the hardships of foreign travel? **(4 marks)**

To revise this question type, see pages 34–36

In **Component 2**, assessment objective 1 will also be used to test your ability to **select information from two texts**. You will need to show your understanding by writing about both texts in your answer.

Assessment objective 2

Assessment objective 2 tests your ability to explain how writers use **language and structure to achieve effects**. You will need to try to use the correct term for the language or structural features in the text.

These are examples of the types of question that will be used to test this skill.

A2 How does the writer suggest that Manderley has been left untouched for a long time? **(5 marks)**

A2 The writer is trying to entertain the reader with her story of travelling with her young daughter. How does she do this? **(10 marks)**

You should comment on:

- what she says to entertain her readers
- what language and tone she uses
- the way she structures her story.

To revise these question types, see pages 17–24

Now try this

What is the main difference between identifying information (assessment objective 1) and explaining how writers use language (assessment objective 2)?

Reading questions explained 2

You will need to answer certain **types of question** in the exam. The questions on this page are sample questions and do not need to be answered.

Assessment objective 3

Assessment objective 3 tests your ability to compare the views put forward in the two non-fiction texts in **Component 2: Section A – Reading**. You will also need to compare the techniques used by the two writers.

This is an example of the type of question that will be used to test this skill.

To answer the following question you will need to use both texts.

A6 Both of these texts are about foreign travel.
Compare the following:
- the writers' attitudes to foreign travel and the places they visit
- how they put across their feelings.

(10 marks)

To revise these question types, see pages 38–42

Questions beginning with 'A' appear in Section A, Reading.

A5 'In the last twenty lines the writer encourages the reader to view the narrator as brave and heroic.'
To what extent do you agree with this view?
You should write about:
- your own impressions of the narrator as he is presented here and in the passage as a whole
- how the writer has created these impressions. **(10 marks)**

A4 What do you think about the writer's feelings about his experiences in Sydney?
You should comment on:
- what he writes
- the way that he writes. **(10 marks)**

To revise these question types, see pages 43–47

These are examples of the type of question that will be used to test this skill.

Assessment objective 4

Assessment objective 4 tests your ability to evaluate texts. This means explaining the ideas and points of view expressed by the writer.

You will need to use appropriate quotations to support your views. You will be able to give your own opinion, but only if you back this up with a solid explanation that relates closely to the text.

Getting it right

Read the questions carefully to make sure you refer to the correct section of the text:
- For **Component 1** each question will tell you which lines of the text to focus on in your answer.
- For **Component 2**, unless the question directs you to particular line numbers, you will need to draw on the whole text for your answer.

Now try this

Look back at the exam-style questions on this page. Circle or highlight the ones that require you to use only a certain part of the text.

Reading the questions

You need to read each question on the exam paper very carefully to make sure you know exactly what it is asking you to do. This page will help you practise how to focus on the **key words in questions.** Do not try to answer the exam questions on this page – focus on picking out key words and fully understanding the question.

Component 1

Read lines 1–14.

A1 List four reasons why the narrator feels his childhood was happy. **(4 marks)**

Check which lines you are being asked to write about.

Identify how many pieces of information you are being asked to find.

Do not explain here. You are only being asked to find and list the reasons.

Check which lines you are being asked to write about.

Pick out the key words in the question. Make sure you use them in your answer.

Use bullet points like these to help you structure your answer.

Here, you will need to give **examples** and **explain the effects** in detail.

You must explain **how** the writer achieves these **effects.**

Component 1

Read lines 1–8.

A4 How does the writer make these lines tense and dramatic? **(10 marks)**

You should write about:

- what happens to build tension
- the writer's use of language and structure to create tension and drama
- the effects on the reader.

Component 2

A4 To answer the following question you will need to read the extract provided.

What do you think and feel about John Crace's view of teenagers?

You should comment on:

- what is said
- how it is said. **(10 marks)**

You must refer to the text to support your comments.

No line numbers are given, so you need to use the whole extract for your answer.

Check if you should write about the whole text or just one specific part of it.

Use bullet points like these to help you structure your answer.

Give **examples** to support your views.

Now try this

Look at the exam-style question on the right.

- How many of the two texts should you write about?
- How much of each text should you use for your answer?
- What are the key words in the question?
- How long should you spend on this question?

This is a **Component 2** question

A6 Both of these texts are about how to treat children and young people.

Compare the following:

- the writers' attitude to children and young people
- how they get across their arguments. **(10 marks)**

You must use the text to support your comments and make it clear which texts you are referring to.

Had a look ☐ Nearly there ☐ Nailed it! ☐

Skimming for the main idea or theme

Maximise the time available in the exam by **skim reading**. First, skim the texts for their main idea or theme. Then follow up with a second, more detailed reading. In particular, skimming will help you with the **non-fiction** extracts in **Component 2**.

Key features

Look at these key places when you skim read a text.

The heading.

The first sentence of each paragraph.

The last sentence of the text.

Summing up

Think about how you could sum up the text in one or two sentences.
Here are some ideas for the text on the right:

Modern teenagers are not interested in paper rounds.

The teenagers of today are lazy and have easier ways of making money than paper rounds.

Who'd Be a Paper Boy?

It's cold, it's dark and you've got to bolt your breakfast before dragging a bag full of papers round the streets. To add insult to injury, you then have to go to school. So who would be bothered with a paper round? Almost no one these days, it seems…

New research from the Cartoon Network shows that your average kid is raking in £770 a year, of which only £32 comes from paper rounds. Which rather suggests that most teenagers last only about a week and a half in the job before finding it a bit much…

And if the little darlings can't stretch to a please and thank you, they can always flog a few household items on eBay. Failing that, there's always the tooth fairy.

Getting it right

To make your skim reading even more useful, read the questions carefully first. The questions will give you clues about the main ideas or themes in the texts.

In the exam, read the question and skim read the text first. Then read the text again in more detail and annotate it with your ideas.

Remember to look at:
- the heading
- the first sentence of each paragraph
- the last sentence of the article.

Now try this

Give yourself 30 seconds to skim read the article *The History of London's Black Cabs* on page 102. Can you sum up the main idea or theme in **one** sentence, or at most **two**?

Annotating the texts

For **both components**, get into the habit of **highlighting, underlining or circling** parts of a text that you can use to support your answers. Then write a note to yourself about why it will be useful in supporting your response. This is called annotating.

Have a look at this question and the annotated extract below.

Read lines 9–17.

A4 How does the writer make these lines tense and dramatic?

You should write about:

- what happens to build tension
- the writer's use of language and structure to create tension and drama
- the effects on the reader. **(10 marks)**

Getting ready to annotate

Before you start annotating:

- ✓ check which lines you need to write about
- ✓ pick out the key words in the question – this will keep your annotations focused
- ✓ look carefully at the bullet points – these will help you know what to look for in the text.

Getting it right

Do not just highlight useful quotes. For each highlight, note down:

- the effect on the reader
- the technique used to achieve it.

Try to use the correct technical language if you know it.

Gathering information for your answer

Highlight features of the text that will be useful in composing your answer.

Extract from Every Man for Himself.
Full text on page 97. Lines 9–13.

As the ship staggered and tipped, a great volume of water flowed in over the submerged bows and tossed me like a cork to the roof. Hopper was there too. My fingers touched some kind of bolt near the ventilation grille and I grabbed it tight. I filled my lungs with air and fixed my eyes on the blurred horizon, determined to hang on until I was sure I could float free rather than be swilled back and forth in a maelstrom.

Emotive language – shows extent of danger

Simile – suggests narrator is helpless

Can't see properly – increases danger

Suggests he has no control

Now try this

Read the extract from *Every Man for Himself* (lines 13–17) on the right.

Highlight, underline or circle any words or phrases that you thin k you could use to answer the exam-style question at the top of this page.

Remember to make a note of the effect that each highlighted word or phrase has on the reader, and the technique that is used to achieve that effect.

I wouldn't waste my strength in swimming, not yet, for I knew the ship was now my enemy and if I wasn't vigilant would drag me with her to the grave. I waited for the next slithering dip and when it came and the waves rushed in and swept me higher, I released my grip and let myself be carried away, over the tangle of ropes and wires and davits, clear of the rails and out into the darkness.

Had a look ☐ Nearly there ☐ Nailed it! ☐

Putting it into practice

In **Component 1: Section A – Reading,** you will need to respond to how writers use **language for effect** in a **fiction** text. Read the extract from *Every Man for Himself* on page 97. Then read the exam-style question below and look at how two students have selected sections of text to help them write an answer.

Commenting on language

For a question like this you should:

- spend about 12 minutes on your answer
- highlight key words in the question so that you get the focus right
- use only the lines of text referred to in the question
- focus on the way the writer has used words and sentences to create ideas about the narrator in the mind of the reader.

Worked example

Read lines 1–17.

A3 What impression do you get of the narrator from these lines? **(10 marks)**

You must refer to the text to support your answer.

Sample answer extract

The narrator is trying hard to survive and he tries to climb to the roof. He is probably brave because he is ready to 'leap for it' and he has lost his friend. However, the water is too powerful for him.

Some useful parts of the text are selected but the student's annotations are not detailed enough. As a result, this answer is not focused and doesn't explain the points very clearly.

… I tried to climb to the roof…	Trying hard
I thought I must make a leap for it…	Probably brave
… turned to look for Hopper	Has lost friend
… then the water, first slithering, then tumbling, gushed us apart.	Water is too powerful

Improved sample answer

The narrator is presented as very determined, as he is 'clinging' to the ladder even though he is unsteady, 'like a flag on a pole'. This gives the impression that he is trying hard in difficult circumstances. He is prepared to 'make a leap for it', which suggests that he is brave, and he is a good friend, checking on his friends – Hopper and Scurra – and putting them first. The words 'some inner voice' suggest he has good instincts under pressure.

Clinging… I tried to climb to the roof… waved like a flag on a pole	Determined, tries even though unsteady
I thought I must make a leap for it…	'Leap' suggests he is brave
… turned to look for Hopper… saw Scurra again, one arm hooked through the rail to steady himself.	Checks on friends, puts others first
… some inner voice…	Has good instincts under pressure

The more focused annotations in this answer extract lead to a more focused, detailed response. Take the time to annotate the text to help you write a stronger answer.

Now try this

Complete the 'Improved sample answer' above. Identify at least **two** more relevant points.

Putting it into practice

In **Component 2: Section A – Reading**, you'll need to respond to how writers use **language for effect** in **non-fiction** texts. Read the extract from *Victorian Cab Drivers* on page 103. Then read the exam-style question below and look at how two students have selected sections of the text to help them write an answer.

Worked example

A4 What do you think about the writer's views about London cab drivers?

You should comment on:

- what is said
- how it is said. **(10 marks)**

You must refer to the text to support your comments.

Focusing on ideas and point of view

For a question like this you should:

- ✓ spend about 12 minutes on your answer
- ✓ highlight/underline key words in the question so that you get the focus right
- ✓ focus on the way the ideas and point of view are expressed by the writer.

Note how the sample answer extract below doesn't focus fully on the key words in the question ('writer's views', 'what', 'how'). Not all of the points given are made relevant to the question. Some points are useful but not explained in detail or linked to a clear statement about the writer's conclusions about what he observes.

Sample answer extract

The writer sees the cab drivers in the mornings, 'after breakfast' and he thinks they are happy. He notices that they drink 'a little more than is quite good' and that they can sleep during the day and eat outside.

When I go and look at them after breakfast…

… the cabman's lot in life is not an unhappy one.

… a little more than is quite good for him to drink

… go to sleep…

… an al fresco [outdoor] dining-table.

Improved sample answer

The writer thinks the cab drivers are happy in their working lives. He reflects that 'the cabman's lot in life is not an unhappy one' and goes on to give examples of the life working outside and being comfortable in the cab. He dismisses the cab drivers' complaints about hunger with 'though', and turns the focus to his view that they drink 'a little more than is quite good' for them. The writer mentions eating twice and the reference to 'an al fresco [outdoor] dining-table' suggests that he feels they spend too much time relaxing.

… the cabman's lot in life is not an unhappy one… he lives out in the open air… sleeps comfortably on his box, and if it rains he can get inside the carriage.

… hardly enough to eat… a little more than is quite good for him to drink.

… an al fresco [outdoor] dining-table.

Note how this answer extract focuses on the key words in the question.

Now try this

Complete the 'Improved sample answer' on *Victorian Cab Drivers* above. Aim to identify at least **three** more relevant points.

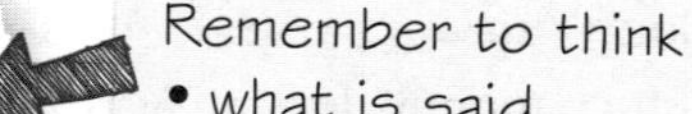

Remember to think about:

- what is said
- how it is said.

Had a look ☐ Nearly there ☐ Nailed it! ☐

Explicit information and ideas

In **Component 2: Section A – Reading** you will be tested on whether you fully understand the writer's main topic. You will need to respond to short questions that ask you to identify **explicit** information and ideas.

'Explicit' means you will not be required to look for **hidden meanings**. You will just need to find **short quotes** or **paraphrase** (put into your own words) what is clearly there.

explicit *adjective*

1. Stated clearly and in detail, leaving no room for confusion or doubt

'the arrangement had not been made explicit'

Synonyms: clear, direct, plain, obvious, straightforward, clear-cut, crystal clear, clearly expressed, easily understandable, blunt

This Component 1 exam-style question is about *Who'd be a Paper Boy?*

Extract from Who'd Be a Paper Boy?
Full text on page 100. Lines 16–24.

'I stopped deliveries 18 months ago,' says Neesa, who just happens to run Costcutter at the top of my road. 'I had four boys earning £20 a week for delivering about 18 papers each per day, and every day at least one would fail to turn up and I'd have to deliver the papers myself to stop customers getting angry. It was just more trouble than it was worth.'

Worked example

A1 (a) When did Neesa stop delivering newspapers? **(1 mark)**

18 months ago.

(b) How much were the four boys earning? **(1 mark)**

£20 per week.

(c) What happened when they failed to turn up? **(1 mark)**

Neesa had to deliver the papers herself.

These questions are asking you to find 'explicit' (clear or obvious) information. Look at the extract on the right to see which sections provide each piece of information.

Getting it right

For the 1-mark questions on the 21st-century text in **Component 2: Section A – Reading**, you only need to give **explicit information**. You do not need to provide any explanation or quotations. Keep your answers as brief as possible – you do not need to waste time writing in full sentences!

18 months ago. ✓

Neesa stopped delivering newspapers 18 months ago. ✗

The text says 'I stopped deliveries 18 months ago,' so Neesa stopped delivering newspapers 18 months ago. ✗

Now try this

You will need to look at the extract from *Who'd Be a Paper Boy?* on page 100 to answer these questions.

1 How long ago was a paper round worth doing? **(1 mark)**
2 How much money does an average child get per year? **(1 mark)**
3 Which TV company has researched children's pocket money? **(1 mark)**

Implicit ideas

For the first question on the 20th-century fiction extract in **Component 1: Section A - Reading**, you will be required to identify both **explicit and implicit** information and ideas.

implicit *adjective*
1. Suggested though not directly expressed
'comments seen as implicit criticism of the children'
Synonyms: implied, indirect, inferred, understood, hinted, suggested, deducible

Reading between the lines

Writers do not always state their meaning explicitly. Sometimes you will have to work out what the writer is **suggesting** or **implying** – in other words, what is **implicit** in the text. This is sometimes called **making an inference** and is also referred to as **reading between the lines**.

Using inference to find implicit meaning

Suggests they didn't know they were different.

Implies their father made their life happy despite prejudice surrounding them.

Suggests that the narrator can now see that something was wrong in his childhood.

Extract from My Son's Story. *Full text on page 98. Lines 1–2.*

We didn't have any particular sense of what we were – my sister and I. I mean, my father made of the circumscription of our life within the areas open to us a charmed circle. Of a kind.

Extract from My Son's Story. *Full text on page 98. Lines 6–9.*

My sister had dancing lessons and he taught me to play chess. I was allowed to stay up quite late on Friday night – no school next day – and we'd sit at the table in the kitchen after supper was cleared away, his great black eyes on me, encouraging, serious…

Inference has been used here to work out the implicit idea in the extract. The fact that the narrator was allowed to stay up late and the table was cleared after supper suggests his father thought chess was an important activity, and his 'encouraging' and 'serious' eyes also imply he was going to pay mature attention to his son rather than treat it like a childish game.

This Component 1 exam-style question is about *My Son's Story*.

Worked example

Read lines 6–9.

A1 List **three** ways in which the narrator's father made their childhood happy. **(3 marks)**

1. He paid for dancing lessons. — Explicit
2. He taught the narrator to play chess. — Explicit
3. He treated the narrator like a grown-up. — Implicit

Now try this

Read the full extract from *My Son's Story* on page 98. Find **four** more ways in which the narrator's father made the children's childhood happy.

Try to keep your answers very brief. Remember that short questions on explicit and implicit information are only worth 1 mark for each point you make! Exact quotes are not always necessary. You can paraphrase instead.

Inference

In **both components**, you will need to make **inferences** (read between the lines) when a question asks you about the feelings, thoughts, views and actions of the writer, or the people or places they are writing about. Remember, inference is about working out what the writer is **implying** (suggesting).

What is the writer implying?

Extract from Rebecca. *Full text on page 96.*
Lines 1–5.

Last night I dreamt I went to Manderley again. It seemed to me I stood by the iron gate leading to the drive, and for a while I could not enter, for the way was barred to me. There was a padlock and a chain upon the gate. I called in my dream to the lodge-keeper, and had no answer, and peering closer through the rusted spokes of the gate I saw that the lodge was uninhabited.

Manderley is an important place as it features in regular dreams.

Suggests it is strongly protected and difficult to enter.

Suggests it has been empty for a while.

This Component 1 exam-style question is about *Rebecca*.

Worked example

Read lines 1–14.

A3 What impression of Manderley do you get from these lines? **(10 marks)**

You must refer to the text to support your answer.

The first line suggests Manderley is an important place as the narrator has dreamt of it again. 'The iron gate' that is 'barred' to the narrator and padlocked suggests that Manderley is strongly protected and difficult to enter. The narrator sees that it is uninhabited and the fact that the spokes are 'rusted' suggests it may have been empty for some time. The overall impression given is that Manderley is a forbidding and frightening place and the narrator's dreams could well be nightmares.

Look out for instructions like this. This means your answer needs to include references to or quotations from the text. You can see examples of this in the answer extract below.

A fully developed answer should:

- refer to evidence from the extract
- comment on what can be inferred from this evidence
- develop and summarise the point with further comments or additional information from the text.

Use **one-word quotations** where possible. This makes your inference really clear and specific.

You can find out more about using quotations on page 45

Now try this

Read the next paragraph (lines 6–19) of the extract from *Rebecca* on page 96. Continue the worked example above using **four** short quotations from the new paragraph. Try to develop your answer fully by summing up your whole point.

Remember to keep Question A3 above in mind. Choose quotations that clearly support the inferences you make.

Interpreting information and ideas

You will often need to **interpret** the information and ideas in a text. For **Component 2: Section A – Reading** you will need to interpret the information and ideas in a 19th-century text. Some of the words or phrases in a text like this may be unfamiliar and tricky to interpret. You need to be able to infer the meaning and explain it in your own words.

Understanding unfamiliar words and phrases

When you are asked to explain an unfamiliar word or phrase, read the text **before** and **after** it in the extract. This will give you more information and help you to infer the meaning. Remember that you can use this approach with all kinds of text, not just the more challenging 19th-century ones.

Extract from Victorian Cab Drivers. *Full text on page 103. Lines 14–17.*

There is a great deal of horse-play among these fellows. I observe one old man who is in the habit of going contentedly asleep on his box. It is a favourite device for someone to lift up the body of the cab from the ground, shake it, and let it dash upon the earth.

The word 'horse-play' is followed by an example of a practical joke, so 'horse-play' is likely to mean silly, childish or even dangerous behaviour.

This Component 2 exam-style question is about *Letters from Sydney*.

Extract from Letters from Sydney. *Full text on page 105. Lines 14–19.*

I have had some rankles in my lifetime, but this bangs all. It took me just six weeks to travel 850 miles, part of which was a dense forest, 160 miles through, your only companions being kangaroos, emus, cockatoos, parrots etc, with now and then a black fellow and his family to be seen, stark naked, and about every 50 or 70 miles, a lonely shepherd gunya, or bark hut, in which you can lay on your bed, and count every star there is in the heavens.

Worked example

Read lines 14–19.

A3 (a) What does the writer mean by 'I have had some rankles in my lifetime, but this bangs all' in lines 14–15…? **(1 mark)**

It means the writer has faced many difficulties and problems before in his life, but his current situation is worse than any of them.

The phrase is followed by lots of examples of the problems the narrator has had on his journey. These details help to explain the meaning of the phrase.

Getting it right

Remember to:

- read the text before and after the word or phrase you need to explain – this will help you to infer the meaning
- explain the **whole** word or phrase you are being asked about in your own words
- keep your answers brief – these questions are only worth 1 or 2 marks.

Now try this

Read the extract from *Victorian Cab Drivers* on page 103 and answer the exam-style question below.

A3 (a) What does the writer mean by 'a man of intellectual resources' in line 5? **(1 mark)**

Had a look ☐ Nearly there ☐ Nailed it! ☐

Point – Evidence – Explanation

P-E-E is a technique you can use in your longer answers for **Component 2** to make them clearer and better organised.

1. Make your **point**.
2. Provide **evidence** to support the point.
3. **Explain** how the evidence supports the point.

Getting it right

P-E-E is particularly useful when answering questions that ask you to:
- **comment** on language and structure
- **evaluate** a text
- **compare** texts.

P-E-E in practice

You should use a range of phrases to link your point, evidence and **explanation**.

1. Make your point: The writer uses / The article focuses on
2. Introduce your evidence: For example, / The writer describes / For instance,
3. Introduce your explanation: This gives the impression that / The writer is implying that / This suggests / This shows

Worked example

Read lines 25–31.

A2 How does the writer use language to get across his main ideas? **(5 marks)**

You must refer to the language used in the text to support your answer.

Note this reminder to focus on the language in the text. Look out for this kind of guidance in a question.

Extract from Who'd Be a Paper Boy? *Full text on page 100. Lines 25–31.*

You can have some sympathy for the kids. Standards in literacy and numeracy have fallen so steeply that it can be a real struggle identifying door names and numbers, and the Sunday papers are now so heavy that your averagely obese teenager just doesn't have the strength or stamina for the job.

The writer mixes serious points with humour. For instance, his point about standards falling 'steeply' is serious but then he jokes that this means teenagers cannot even identify 'door names and numbers'. By making a serious point in an entertaining way, the writer is able to engage as well as inform readers.

- The paragraph opens with a detailed point that addresses the question.
- The linking phrase 'for instance' shows clearly that evidence will be used and two quotations are given.
- The evidence is then explained in detail with a comment on the effect of the language on the reader.

Now try this

Read the text extract from *Who'd Be a Paper Boy?* Full text on page 100. Lines 1–4.

Choose a short quotation to support the following point: 'The writer uses negative language to make paper rounds appear unappealing.'

It's cold, it's dark and you've got to bolt your breakfast before dragging a bag full of papers round the streets.

Putting it into practice

In **Component 1: Section A – Reading**, you'll need to respond to how a writer uses **language and structure** to achieve particular **effects**. Read the extract from *Every Man for Himself* on page 97. Then look at the exam-style question below and read the extracts from two students' answers.

Commenting on language and structure

For a question like this you should:

- ✓ spend about 12 minutes on your answer
- ✓ read the question carefully and **highlight the main focus**
- ✓ only use the lines of text **referred to in the question**
- ✓ comment on **how** the writer uses language and structure and what the **effects** are on the reader.

Worked example

Read lines 9–23.

A4 How does the writer suggest that the narrator is brave?

You should write about:

- what happens to suggest he is brave
- the writer's use of language and structure to suggest bravery
- the effects on the reader. **(10 marks)**

Remember to read the question and skim read the text first. Then read the text again in more detail, and annotate it with your ideas.

Sample answer extract

The ship 'staggered and tipped' and the narrator is 'tossed' 'like a cork' so this suggests he is brave.

The narrator also appears to be brave because he is able to grab a bolt even though he is under the water. He then takes action by filling his lungs and fixing his eyes as he is 'determined' to save himself.

✗ Although this uses quotations, there is no clear point and the sentence does not focus clearly on the question.

✓ This has a clear point and refers to the text, although the second sentence does not really develop into an explanation of any of the evidence.

You should use P-E-E to help you structure your answer so that it includes a clear explanation of how your evidence supports your point.

Improved sample answer

The writer encourages the reader to feel the narrator is brave by starting the paragraph with details of the danger he is in. For instance, the narrator is tossed 'like a cork' which suggests he may be hurt but he is then able to grab 'some kind of bolt'. This shows that he remains calm despite the danger he is in, this is a sign of bravery.

✓ Clear point that refers directly to the question.

✓ Use of linking phrase 'for instance' signals clear use of relevant quotes.

✓ Fully developed explanation that refers back to the question.

Note how this answer refers directly to the effect of the writer's choices on the reader.

Now try this

Complete the 'Improved sample answer' on *Every Man for Himself* above. Aim to identify and explain **three** more relevant points.

Use a clear P-E-E structure to make your answer clear and focused on the question.

Putting it into practice

In **Component 2: Section A – Reading**, you'll need to respond to how a writer uses **language and structure** for **effect**. Read the extract from *The History of London's Black Cabs* on page 102. Then look at the exam-style question below and read the extracts from two students' answers.

Worked example

A2 The writer is trying to show us how difficult it is to be a London cab driver. How does he try to do this?

You should comment on:

- what he says to influence readers
- his use of language and tone
- the way he presents his argument. **(10 marks)**

Commenting on language and structure

For a question like this you should:

- ✓ spend about 12 minutes on your answer
- ✓ read the question carefully and **highlight the main focus**
- ✓ only use the lines of the text **referred to in the question**
- ✓ comment on **how** the writer uses language and structure and what the **effects** are on the reader.

Sample answer extract

The writer shows being a London cab driver is difficult as the writer can't even open the doors to start with, and panics when two passengers get into his cab.

He also doesn't know where to go as his nerves are 'frayed'.

✓ Clear introduction that refers to the question, although the explanation is not really clear at the end of the sentence.

✗ This section only gives evidence without making a point or explaining the effect of the writer's use of language.

Remember that P-E-E stands for **Point – Evidence – Explain**. You need to include an explanation to make your answer complete and effective.

Improved sample answer

The writer shows being a London cab driver is difficult as the writer can't even open the doors to start with, and he panics when he gets his first two passengers. This suggests that it is a nerve-racking job that probably requires proper training. The writer then goes on to say that his nerves are 'frayed', and he makes a joke by calling the destination 'Tuxedo Junction'. This suggests that the job of a cab driver is difficult, as it has made him very nervous and unable even to think about the correct route.

✓ Clear introduction that refers to the question, followed by clear evidence from the text

✓ Use of linking phrase 'This suggests' clearly signals an explanation

✓ Further examples are provided of the writer's choice of language and tone

✓ Clear and fully developed explanation that links back to the question

Now try this

Complete the 'Improved sample answer' on *The History of London's Black Cabs* above. Aim to identify and explain **three** more relevant points.

Remember to:

- focus on the key points in the question
- make a clear point
- use evidence from the text to support your point
- explain how the evidence you use supports your point.

Word classes

In **both components** you will be asked to comment on the writers' **choice of language**. Start by thinking about the types of word – or **word classes** – writers use.

Nouns

These are words used to describe:

- objects (duck, sandwich, gate, chimney)
- people (bloke, park-keeper, Marcus, father)
- places (Manderley, town, country)
- ideas (keenness, health, encouragement).

Verbs

These are words used to describe:

- actions (to throw, to hit, to nod)
- occurrences (to fail, to retire)
- states (to be, to think, to dream).

Remember: **pronouns** such as 'he', 'they', 'it' can replace or stand in for **nouns**.

Adjectives

These are words used to describe a noun. Examples are 'tatty', 'supernatural', 'small', 'long', 'dark'.

Remember: **adjectives** can become **comparatives** (e.g. 'longer', 'darker') and **superlatives** (e.g. 'longest', 'darkest).

Adverbs

These are words which describe verbs. They are usually formed by adding 'ly' to an adjective. Examples are 'unhappily', 'frantically', 'badly', 'generally', 'often', 'sometimes'.
Adverbs can also modify adjectives and other adverbs.

Getting it right

Make sure you are familiar with these **adjective** forms and how to use them:
Comparatives describe degrees of difference, e.g. 'smaller', 'longer', 'darker', 'more dangerous'.
Superlatives describe the most or least, e.g. 'smallest', 'longest', 'darkest', 'most dangerous'.

Examples

Here are some sample student comments about the extracts opposite, focusing on word class:

1 Clinging to the rung of the ladder I tried to climb to the roof but there was such a sideways slant that I waved like a flag on a pole.

The writer uses five verbs in the sentence to focus the reader's mind on the danger faced by the narrator.

2 What did it matter that the seaside hotels, the beaches, pleasure-grounds with swimming pools were not for us?

The writer uses a list of nouns to emphasise how much discrimination the narrator faces.

3 What say you, then, of children-children of the tenderest years? Why, they become stunted, crippled, deformed, useless.

The writer uses strong adjectives in a list, and a superlative ('tenderest'), to create a vivid picture.

Now try this

Read the first paragraph (lines 1–8) of the extract from *Every Man for Himself* on page 97.
Write **two** sentences focusing on the writer's use of word class and its effect.

Had a look ☐ Nearly there ☐ Nailed it! ☐

Connotations

Some words can create bigger ideas in our minds through the ideas and attitudes they suggest. These ideas and attitudes are called **connotations**.

Thinking about what a word or phrase suggests can help you to write effective comments on the writer's choice of language in **both components**.

Look at what the phrase 'angry roaring' could suggest in the example opposite.

... the angry roaring of the dying ship...

The connotation of the phrase 'angry roaring' suggests the ship is like a furious beast. This, in turn, suggests the ship is large and distressed.

Language choice

These sentences have similar literal meanings. But the connotations let you know the writer's **real attitude**.

1. The cold water pulled me down.
2. The icy liquid dragged me down.
3. The Arctic flow sucked me under.

Exploring the **connotations** of the language in a text can help you to write about the **atmosphere** that is created, or about the **attitude** of the writer.

Connotations in context

Words can have different meanings depending on what comes before or after them in a text. You need to think about what comes **before** and **after** – the context – to interpret words correctly and understand their connotations.

context *noun*
The parts of something written or spoken that immediately precede and follow a word or passage and clarify its meaning.

Extract from Every Man for Himself. *Full text on page 97. Lines 1–4.*

The stern began to lift from the water. Guggenheim and his valet played mountaineers, going hand over hand up the rail. The hymn turned ragged; ceased altogether. The musicians scrambled upwards, the spike of the cello scraping the deck.

This literally means people who climb mountains but here it carries connotations of bravery and daring.

This literally means torn and tattered but it also has connotations suggesting broken, uneven and ruined.

This literally means moving quickly and awkwardly but here it also has connotations of being unable to find a footing, and of panic and desperation.

Now try this

Now read lines 1–6 of the extract from *Victorian Child Labour* on page 101.
What are the connotations of these words?

endurance poisonous burden

Write **one** brief sentence to explain the literal meaning and the connotation of **each** word.

Figurative language

For **Component 1** you will need to comment on the way writers use **language** to create **atmosphere** or to make readers feel a particular **emotion**. **Figurative language**, or **imagery**, is often used to create pictures in the reader's mind and make description more vivid.

Comment on figurative language

To improve your exam answers you will need to **explain** the **effect** of figurative language in a text.

Getting it right

When you are commenting on figurative language, make sure you:

- comment on the **effect** of the language used
- give the name for the figurative device used if you know it.

simile *noun*
A figure of speech involving the indirect comparison of one thing to another, usually using 'as' or 'like'

Extract from Every Man for Himself. *Full text on page 97. Lines 9–10.*

As the ship staggered and tipped, a great volume of water flowed in over the submerged bows and tossed me **like** a cork to the roof.

The writer uses a simile to compare the narrator to something very light: a cork. This emphasises the power of the water and makes the narrator seem more vulnerable and defenceless. Corks are also a small, disposable item so it suggests that the narrator is powerless against the force of the water.

metaphor *noun*
A direct comparison suggesting a resemblance between one thing and another

Extract from Rebecca. *Full text on page 96. Line 20.*

The drive **was** a ribbon now, a thread of its former self, with gravel surface gone…

The writer uses a metaphor to compare the drive to a ribbon and a thread. This suggests the drive is no longer solid or capable of carrying vehicles and 'thread' suggests it has become narrow and fragile.

Personification *noun*
Describing something non-human as if it were human

Extract from Rebecca. *Full text on page 96. Lines 15–16.*

The beeches with white, naked limbs leant close to one another, their branches intermingled in a strange embrace…

The writer personifies the trees as strange, ghost-like creatures huddled together; this creates an image of a type of nightmarish army united against the narrator.

Now try this

Read the second paragraph (lines 6–19) of the extract from *Rebecca* on page 96. Identify at least **two** more examples of figurative language. Write **one** or **two** sentences about the effect **each** example is intended to have on the reader.

Remember to comment on the effect of the figurative language, as well as naming the device used if you can.

Had a look ☐ Nearly there ☐ Nailed it! ☐

Creation of character

For **Component 1** you may be asked to comment on the way a writer has used **language** to create a particular **impression** of a **character**.

Character through action

Consider what the character **does** in the extract.

Extract from Every Man for Himself. *Full text on page 97. Lines 21–23.*

I was sucked under, as I knew I would be, down, down, and still I waited, waited until the pull slackened – then I struck out with all my strength.

Verbs are used to show how the narrator waits patiently for the right time to swim, which suggests the character's bravery.

The connotations of 'struck out' are powerful, suggesting the character will try to fight the water.

Also see page 18 for a reminder about connotations

Also see page 17 for a reminder about word classes

Getting it right

Look out for **action** words – **verbs** and **adverbs**.

Extract from My Son's Story. *Full text on page 98. Lines 8–9.*

…his great black eyes on me, encouraging, serious, crinkling into a smile back in their darkness…

Character through description

Look at **how** the writer **describes** the character.

The writer uses adjectives to emphasise how the character is looking closely at the narrator.

'Black' (adjective) and 'darkness' (noun) add to the feeling that he is taking the narrator seriously, but 'crinkling' (verb) suggests that he also has a sense of humour.

Getting it right

Look out for **describing words** (adjectives) and **figurative language**.

Also see page 19 for a reminder about figurative language

Character through dialogue

Think about how **dialogue** is used to build up an idea of the character.

Extract from About a Boy. *Full text on page 99. Lines 23–24.*

'That's not a sandwich, that's a bloody french loaf. No wonder it keeled over. That would have killed me.'

'Oh, Marcus,' Suzie sighed.

Colloquial language is used to create some humour but use of 'bloody' also suggests the character may be a little angry.

The use of 'sighed' rather than 'said' suggests Suzie is disappointed, sad or weary.

Getting it right

Look out for **colloquial** (informal or conversational) **language**.

Now try this

Read lines 25–34 of the extract from *About a Boy* on page 99. Identify **two** more examples of how dialogue is used to create character. Write a P-E-E paragraph for **each** example.

Use technical language where you can to strengthen your response.

Creating atmosphere

For **Component 1** you will need to think about how writers use a wide range of language devices in order to create an **atmosphere**. Sometimes this is called the **mood** or **tone** of a piece of writing. You may also be asked to comment on how a writer presents a setting.

Personification of trees – 'thrown out' makes them seem aggressive and threatening

Metaphor comparing the drive to a ribbon and a thread – suggests the drive is no longer solid or capable of carrying vehicles and 'thread' suggests it has become narrow and fragile

Extract from Rebecca. *Full text on page 96. Lines 20–22.*

The drive was a ribbon now, a thread of its former self, with gravel surface gone, and choked with grass and moss. The trees had thrown out low branches, making an impediment to progress, the gnarled roots looked like skeleton claws.

Verb suggests forceful action – adds to the sense of danger

Personification of drive – 'choked' suggests it is literally being killed

Adjective – suggests age

Simile – creates a sense of death and decay

Connotations of animal strength

Taking an overview

When you have identified the language devices used and their connotations and effects, look at whether the devices work together to create a particular mood or tone. This is called taking an 'overview' and can help you to show the examiner that you fully understand the extract.

The overall tone of the extract above is one of danger and decay.

Getting it right

When you answer a question about language techniques, it is a good idea to start with your 'overview' to sum up the overall effect created by the writer. You can do this by using phrases like these:

Overall, the writer suggests…

Overall, the writer creates…

The overall tone of the extract is…

Now try this

Read the final part (lines 24–38) of the extract from *Rebecca* on page 96. Identify as many language techniques as you can. For **each one**, comment on its effect or connotations. Then take an 'overview'. What overall mood or tone does the writer create?

Narrative voice

For **Component 1: Section 1 – Reading**, you may need to discuss **narrative voice** in your response to a question. (On rare occasions you may also need to do this for narrative non-fiction in **Component 2**.) Narrative voice is the 'voice' a writer of fiction chooses to tell the story. The choice of narrative voice can be used to create a particular **point of view**.

First-person narrative

Extract from Rebecca. *Full text on page 96. Lines 1–5.*

Last night I dreamt I went to Manderley again. It seemed to me I stood by the iron gate leading to the drive, and for a while I could not enter, for the way was barred to me.

A narrative written in the **first person** is told by an **'I'**. The 'I' can be the main character or a less important character witnessing events. This point of view is effective in giving a sense of **closeness to the character** and readers are often encouraged to sympathise with them.

Third-person narrative

Extract from About a Boy. *Full text on page 99. Lines 1–2.*

Marcus couldn't believe it. Dead. A dead duck. OK, he'd been *trying* to hit it on the head with a piece of sandwich, but he *tried* to do all sorts of things, and none of them had ever happened before.

Characters are referred to in the **third person, by their name or as 'he' or 'she'**. In a third-person narrative, the narrator is not a character in the story. Sometimes this type of narrator knows everything, including a character's thoughts; sometimes they only appear to look in from the outside.

In this extract, the third-person narrative is all-knowing. This is called an **omniscient narrator**. This means the reader knows Marcus's **thoughts** and **feelings**. This is a deliberate way of making the reader sympathetic towards Marcus.

Question relating to the text extract from *About a Boy*. Full text on page 99.

Worked example

Read lines 1–7.

A5 In these lines, the writer encourages the reader to feel sympathy for Marcus.
To what extent do you agree with this view?

You should write about:

- your own impressions of Marcus as he is presented here and in the passage as a whole
- how the writer has created these impressions.

(10 marks)

The writer has used third-person omniscient narration to show the reader what Marcus is thinking. He is unable to believe that he has killed a duck despite 'trying' and this suggests that he is pessimistic about his own abilities. This may make a reader feel sympathy towards him.

- Clearly identifies the narrative voice
- Interprets what the narrative voice tells the reader about the character's thoughts and suggests what this reveals about the character
- Suggests the effect on the reader

This is a partial answer. You would need to write more for this question in your exam.

Now try this

Read lines 7–13 of the extract from *About a Boy* on page 99. Write **one** clear P-E-E paragraph commenting on the writer's use of third-person narration and its effects.

Remember, using a P-E-E structure in your answer will help to make your answer clear, focused and fully developed.

Putting it into practice

In **Component 1: Section A – Reading**, you'll need to respond to the **language** in a fiction text. Read the extract from *Rebecca* on page 96. Then look at the exam-style question below and read the extracts from two students' answers.

Writing about language

For a question like this you should:

- spend about 12 minutes on your answer
- read the question carefully and highlight the main focus
- only use the lines of the text referred to in the question
- identify the language devices used and comment on their effects.

Worked example

Read lines 6–19.

A4 How does the writer create a sense of danger and tension in these lines?

You should write about:

- what happens to build tension
- the writer's use of language to create danger and tension
- the effects on the reader. **(10 marks)**

Here the focus is on language but in the exam you will need to write about structure for this type of question, too.

Sample answer extract

The writer personifies nature which is described as having 'fingers'. This suggests that it may reach out and hurt the narrator. The writer also uses the adjective 'stealthy' to describe nature, which makes the reader feel that something hidden or secret may be lurking ahead of the narrator.

✗ No overview at start of *answer*

✗ Identifies language device but no clear point or reference to *question*

✓ Clearly identifies language device and gives an *example*

✓ A clear explanation which includes comment about effect on *reader*

Improved sample answer

Overall, the writer creates a sense of danger and tension by personifying nature as something threatening. Nature is said to have 'long, tenacious fingers' which suggests that it may actually reach out and harm the narrator. Nature is also described using the adjective 'stealthy' which makes the reader feel that something hidden or secret may be lurking ahead of the narrator.

✓ Very clear overview at start of *answer*

✓ Clear quotes and explanation which develop the point made in the overview *sentence*

✓ Clear identification of language device and the word 'also' signals that the point is being fully developed by using more than one piece of *evidence*

Note how the points made in this answer are well developed, and how the evidence from the text is clearly explained.

Now try this

Complete the 'Improved sample answer' on *Rebecca* above. You should aim to identify and explain **three** more relevant points using the following terminology:

connotations | metaphor | verb

Had a look ☐ Nearly there ☐ Nailed it! ☐

Putting it into practice

Read the extract from *My Son's Story* on page 98. Then look at the exam-style question below and read the extracts from two students' answers.

Remember, in this kind of question you need to **explain the effects** of the language the writer uses.

Worked example

Read lines 25–32.

A3 What impressions do you get of the narrator's childhood in these lines? **(10 marks)**

You must refer to the text to support your answer.

Writing about language

For a question like this you should:

- ✓ spend about 12 minutes on your answer
- ✓ read the question carefully and **highlight the main focus**
- ✓ only use the lines of text **referred to in the question**
- ✓ identify the **language devices** used and comment on their **effects**.

Sample answer extract

The writer uses a rhetorical question to highlight that his childhood was still happy despite lack of access to some facilities. The use of 'our kind' and 'no-man's land' then make it seem unhappy. The use of the verb 'picknicked' in the middle of a list of activities the children were allowed to do makes the childhood seem happy.

This answer extract identifies language devices and makes relevant points that focus on the question, but the effects of the devices are not always fully developed. A clear overview and use of P-E-E would help make this answer stronger.

✓ Clear identification of language device with an explanation that refers to the question

✗ Clear relevant quotes but no real explanation of their effect

✓ Clear identification of language device and some explanation

Improved sample answer

Overall the narrator appears to have enjoyed his childhood, although there are hints of resentment about the restrictions caused by apartheid. The writer highlights their childhood happiness by using a rhetorical question. The rhetorical question contains a list of leisure activities barred to the narrator and at first it seems like this shows they didn't mind. However, the following sentence contains the phrases 'our kind' and 'no-man's land' which suggest the narrator did actually care about the activities he was barred from. 'Our kind' suggests he knew he was different even as a child, and 'no man's land' has connotations of war and fighting. These phrases contrast with the 'pleasure-grounds' mentioned in the rhetorical question and suggest that...

The language devices are well selected and their effects clearly explained.

✓ Clear overview, which uses inference to show an understanding of the hidden tension in the extract

✓ Clear identification of technique with comment on effect and use of P-E-E

✓ Inference has been used to explore fully the connotations of quotes selected

Now try this

Complete the final sentence of the 'Improved sample answer' on *My Son's Story* opposite and then make **two** further points in response to the exam-style question. Try to write about the use of the first person as the narrative voice.

For a reminder about narrative voice, see page 22

Rhetorical devices 1

For **Component 2** you will need to think about the range of **language** or **rhetorical devices** that writers use to **emphasise** their points or to **manipulate** the reader's response.

Extract from Who'd Be a Paper Boy? *Full text on page 100. Lines 1–6.*

It's cold, it's dark and you've got to bolt your breakfast before dragging a bag full of papers round the streets. To add insult to injury, you then have to go to school. So who would be bothered with a paper round? Almost no one these days, it seems.

The writer has put a list into a pattern of three to highlight and exaggerate the negative aspects of getting up to do a paper round.

pattern of three: a rhythmic trio of words or phrases used to highlight or exaggerate a point for emphasis

list: series of items or ideas, often used to highlight quantity or variety

The writer has used alliteration to create humour and to emphasise how unappealing paper rounds are to young people.

alliteration: two or more words close to each other that begin with same sound; used for emphasis

Using a rhetorical question in the first paragraph engages the reader, as does the colloquialism 'bothered', and invites them to agree with the answer.

rhetorical question: a question used to engage the reader

colloquialism: informal, conversational word or phrase

Getting it right

Remember to comment on the effect a device has, rather than just naming it. Use the technical name for the device if you know it, but even if you don't, you should still comment on the language and its effect.

Now try this

Read the whole of the extract from *Who'd Be a Paper Boy?* on page 100. Identify as many other examples of rhetorical devices as you can. Write **one** sentence about the effect **each** device is intended to have on the reader.

Remember, you can also identify and comment on the effects of the word classes and figurative language used!

For a reminder about word classes and figurative language see pages 17 and 19

Rhetorical devices 2

Here are some more rhetorical devices you need to be able to recognise and comment on.

Extract from The Hungry Cyclist. *Full text on page 104. Lines 2–9.*

Gasping for breath I said goodbye to a country I had fallen in love with and entered another. From the border, where the usual money changers, pickpockets and disgruntled border officials did everything to make life worse, I rode towards Quito. But in Ecuador it seemed as though someone had dimmed the lights and turned down the volume. Gone were the smiles and friendly cheers of encouragement from the roadside. Gone were the picturesque colonial farmsteads with their flower-covered porches. Here homes were functional, unfinished concrete, spewing construction steel. It rained, it was cold and I wanted to turn around.

The writer uses the verb 'gasping' to make the reader feel sympathy for the narrator, as it suggests he is struggling to breathe.

emotive language: words intended to create an extreme response or play on the reader's emotions

The writer repeatedly contrasts the attractive natural landscape he has left behind with the stark landscape of Ecuador in order to emphasise how unwelcome it appears.

contrast: comparing two opposing or different ideas to emphasise the difference between them

Repeating the word 'gone' emphasises the contrast between the two countries and exaggerates the negative aspects of Ecuador.

repetition: a repeated word or phrase to emphasise an idea

Extract from Who'd Be a Paper Boy? *Full text on page 100. Lines 25–33.*

You can have some sympathy for the kids. Standards in literacy and numeracy have fallen so steeply that it can be a real struggle identifying door names and numbers, and the Sunday papers are now so heavy that your averagely obese teenager just doesn't have the strength or stamina for the job. But the bottom line is that most kids can no longer be bothered to get out of bed for £20.

The writer uses hyperbole to emphasise the laziness of modern teenagers when it comes to earning money.

hyperbole: extreme exaggeration used to make a point

Getting it right

Make sure you are familiar with these rhetorical devices and how they can be used:

- pattern of three
- list
- alliteration
- rhetorical question
- colloquialism
- emotive language
- repetition
- contrast
- hyperbole

Now try this

Read the next paragraph (lines 10–16) of the extract from *The Hungry Cyclist* on page 104 . Identify **two** other examples of rhetorical devices. Write **one** sentence about the way in which **each** device is used to manipulate the response of the reader.

Fact, opinion and expert evidence

For **Component 2** you will need to think about how writers make their ideas more **persuasive** or **convincing** by supporting them with **facts, opinions** and **expert evidence**.

Getting it right

Referring to how the writer has used facts, opinions and expert evidence can improve your answers.

fact
Something that can be **proved** to be true.
Example: *'Manchester is a city in the United Kingdom.'*

opinion
An idea or viewpoint that the writer or speaker **believes** to be true.
Example: *'Manchester is the greatest city on earth.'*

expert evidence
Facts or opinions provided by an expert on the subject.
Example: *'Barry Chesham, a travel writer with over 30 years' experience, says: "Manchester is the greatest city on earth."'*

Extract from Who'd Be a Paper Boy? *Full text on page 100. Lines 25–44.*

You can have some sympathy for the kids. Standards in literacy and numeracy have fallen so steeply that it can be a real struggle identifying door names and numbers, and the Sunday papers are now so heavy that your averagely obese teenager just doesn't have the strength or stamina for the job. But the bottom line is that most kids can no longer be bothered to get out of bed for £20.

New research from the Cartoon Network shows that your average kid is raking in £770 a year, of which only £32 comes from paper rounds. Which rather suggests that most teenagers last only about a week and a half in the job before finding it a bit much.

The bulk of the cash comes from pocket money (£186) and part-time work (£256) – selling fags outside the school gates, presumably – but the most telling items are for performance-related pay.

Read the extract on the right. In this article the writer:

- makes his viewpoint clear by giving his **opinion**
- refers to **expert evidence** to back up his opinion
- supports his opinion with more **facts and statistics**.

Now try this

Read the text extract *Who'd Be a Paper Boy?* on page 100. Note down **one** further **fact**, **one** further **opinion** and **one** further piece of **expert evidence** that the writer uses to support his viewpoint.

Make sure you know the difference between a fact, an opinion and expert evidence.

Had a look ☐ Nearly there ☐ Nailed it! ☐

Identifying sentence types

For **both components** you will need to comment on the types of sentences a writer uses to **create effects** and **influence** the reader.

Single-clause sentences

Single-clauses sentences (sometimes called simple sentences) are made up of just **one clause** (a unit of information) and provide **one piece of information** about an event or action.

They contain a subject and **one verb**. For example:

Marcus threw the sandwich.

This is the verb.

Subordinate clauses

A **subordinate clause** does not make sense on its own. It is **dependent** on the main clause. For example:

This is the main clause.

Marcus threw the sandwich because he was bored.

This is the subordinate clause.

Note how the two clauses are joined with conjunctions such as **until**, **although** and **if**. In the above example, the conjunction is **because**.

Sometimes, the clauses in a multi-clause sentence can be swapped round. For example:

Because he was bored, Marcus threw the sandwich.

Coordinate clauses

Clauses are **coordinate** if they are an **equal** pair – in other words, neither clause is dependent on the other. For example:

'Marcus threw the sandwich' and 'hit a duck.'

These clauses are linked as an equal pair.

Note how the two clauses are joined with conjunctions such as **and**, **but** and **then**. In this example, the conjunction is **and**.

Multi-clause sentences

Multi-clause sentences (sometimes called compound and complex sentences) are made up of **more than one clause**. They contain **two or more verbs**.

Minor sentences

These are grammatically incomplete because they do not contain a verb. For example:

Poor duck. A sandwich.

Not fair!

Now try this

What kinds of sentence are these? How do you know?

1 Because the sandwich hit the duck, the duck died.
2 It sank like a stone.
3 The park-keeper arrived at the scene and questioned Marcus intensely.
4 Dead.

Commenting on sentence types

How writers **structure a sentence** can have just as much impact on the reader as the language they choose. This is true for both **fiction (Component 1)** and **non-fiction (Component 2)** texts.

Long sentences

A longer multi-clause sentence with several subordinate clauses can be used in many ways, for example to create tension or atmosphere, or for emphasis. This type of sentence is most commonly used in texts aimed at adults.

Extract from Victorian Child Labour. *Full text on page 101. Lines 2–4.*

But what say you, my Lords, to a continuity of toil, in a standing posture, in a poisonous atmosphere, during 13 hours, with 15 minutes of rest?

The addition of several additional clauses builds up the main point the speaker is making. This is particularly effective in a speech.

Extract from Rebecca. *Full text on page 96. Lines 17–19.*

And there were other trees as well, trees that I did not recognise, squat oaks and tortured elms that straggled cheek by jowl with the beeches, and had thrust themselves out of the quiet earth, along with monster shrubs and plants, none of which I remembered.

This long sentence creates a tense mood as it builds up a vivid picture of the trees in the mind of the reader. Each extra clause adds another layer to the imagery.

Short sentences

Short, single-clause sentences are associated with texts for children, but can also be used in texts aimed at adults, to create drama or to mimic a narrator's or writer's thoughts.

Extracts from About a Boy. *Full text on page 99. Lines 1 and 26.*

Marcus couldn't believe it. Dead. A dead duck.

Marcus hated him even more. Who did this Will think he was?

These short sentences reflect Marcus's thoughts. They are short because he is worried and angry.

Long and short sentences

Putting a short sentence after a long sentence can increase the dramatic effect. A final short sentence can also be used to sum up or to contrast the content of the longer sentence that comes before it.

Extract from My Son's Story. *Full text on page 98. Lines 29–32.*

There, on our rug, overseen by nobody, safe from everybody, the drunks next door and the municipality in the town, my father would lay his head in my mother's lap and we children would lie against their sides, under the warmth of their arms. A happy childhood.

The final sentence is short as it is used to sum up and emphasise the happiness that has been described in detail in the longer sentence before it.

Now try this

Read the extract from *My Son's Story* on page 98, focusing on the final **two** sentences. Write **one** or **two** sentences explaining the effect created by the use of two short sentences at this point in the extract.

Remember that you do not need to quote whole sentences in your answers! It is enough to refer to them like this: 'the use of a short sentence' or 'the effect of the long multi-clause sentence about…'.

Structure: non-fiction

The **overall structure** of non-fiction texts can be used by writers to create a **particular tone**, to **structure** a text for a particular **purpose** or to **manipulate** the reader's response. You will need to explore this for **Component 2**.

Opening

The opening of any text needs to **engage** the attention of the reader. In a non-fiction text, the opening, or **introduction**, can be used to set the scene, like the example on the right.

Starts on a personal note with information about his life and disability – engages the sympathy of the reader and makes them want to continue reading.

Extract from Victorian Cab Drivers. *Full text on page 103. Lines 1–4 and line 10.*

For some little time I have been confined to the house. Instead of going abroad after breakfast, I stay in the dining-room, and I generally manage to limp to the dining-room windows. Now just opposite these windows is a cabstand. I used to think that cabstand a nuisance, but the truth now dawns upon me that there is compensation in most things.

When I go and look at them after breakfast…

Development

The main, middle section of a text needs to hold the reader's interest so that they keep reading. This is often achieved by **changing the tone** or by creating a **contrasting argument**, as in the example below. The middle section can also be used to **develop an argument** or to give a more **detailed explanation** of the main point.

This pair of short, grammatically incorrect sentences in the middle of the text:

- signals that the tone of the writing is about to change
- creates an informal tone which makes it feel like the writer is having a conversation with the reader.

Extract from The Hungry Cyclist. *Full text on page 104. Lines 14–18.*

Not at all tempted by the usual suspects that made up the options in these small Ecuadorian towns, I began to wonder if my hunger could hold out until breakfast.

But hello! What's this?

Conclusion

Writers need to leave readers with a lasting impression. Ending styles can include: vivid images, warnings, calls to action, positivity or a summary of the main points made.

This speech ends on a positive note, as the speakers' laws have worked in Bradford. This will make listeners believe that the terrible suffering can be prevented in the future.

Picks up the purpose of the conclusion of this speech – to rally and inspire the audience.

Extract from Victorian Child Labour. *Full text on page 101. Lines 13–16.*

This was the effect of prolonged toil on the tender frames of children at early ages. When I visited Bradford, under the limitation of hours some years afterwards, I called for a similar exhibition of cripples; but, God be praised! There was not one to be found in that vast city. Yet the work of these poor sufferers had been light, if measured by minutes, but terrific when measured by hours.

Now try this

Read the extract from *Letters from Sydney* on page 105. Pay particular attention to the final paragraph of the letter and then write a sentence commenting on the structure of the text. What does it reveal about the feelings of the writer?

Think about the structural choices the writer has made and what effects these choices have.

Structure: fiction

Structure is also important when commenting on a **fiction** text. Writers of **fiction** use a variety of **narrative structures** to achieve particular effects. You will need to explore this for **Component 1**.

Foreshadowing

foreshadowing *noun*
An advance sign or warning of what is to come in the future. The author of a mystery novel might use foreshadowing in an early chapter of their book to give readers an inkling of an impending murder.

Extract from Rebecca. *Full text on page 96. Lines 1–6.*

Last night I dreamt I went to Manderley again. It seemed to me I stood by the iron gate leading to the drive, and for a while I could not enter, for the way was barred to me. There was a padlock and a chain upon the gate. I called in my dream to the lodge-keeper, and had no answer, and peering closer through the rusted spokes of the gate I saw that the lodge was uninhabited. No smoke came from the chimney, and the little lattice windows gaped forlorn.

The tense and dramatic atmosphere later in the extract is foreshadowed by the many references to Manderley being locked and empty, and to the narrator's way being barred.

Use of closely described detail or action

Describing detail or action closely can suggest time dragging or it can focus a reader's mind on the event taking place, giving it a sense of great importance.

Extract from Every Man for Himself. *Full text on page 97. Lines 13–17.*

I wouldn't waste my strength in swimming, not yet, for I knew the ship was now my enemy and if I wasn't vigilant would drag me with her to the grave. I waited for the next slithering dip and when it came and the waves rushed in and swept me higher, I released my grip and let myself be carried away, over the tangle of ropes and wires and davits, clear of the rails and out into the darkness.

Here the detail about the narrator's thoughts and actions, and the close descriptions of the ship and the water, highlight both the danger he is in, and his bravery.

Repetition and dialogue

Repetition can be used to stress the importance of a word or phrase, or to highlight an idea. Dialogue (or direct speech) can be used to give readers greater insight into characters, and to show how characters interact with one another.

Also see page 20 for a reminder of how dialogue can be used to create character

Extract from About a Boy. *Full text on page 99. Lines 19–20.*

'Maybe someone saw you, or definitely? Maybe they said they were going to get the park-keeper, or definitely?' Marcus didn't like this bloke, so he didn't answer him.

The sarcastic repetition of 'maybe' suggests the speaker is angry and an adult reader might feel that it shows he does not understand children.

The direct speech used here allows the reader to see how characters interact, and allows more of Marcus's feelings and thoughts to be shown.

Now try this

Read lines 17–23 of the extract from *Every Man for Himself* on page 97. Write **one** or **two** sentences commenting on the writer's use of structure and its effects.

Had a look ☐ Nearly there ☐ Nailed it! ☐

Putting it into practice

In **Component 1: Section A – Reading**, you'll need to respond to the **language** and **structure** in a **fiction** text. Read the extract from *About a Boy* on page 99. Then look at the exam-style question below and read the extracts from two students' answers.

Worked example

Read lines 21–35.

A4 How does the writer make these lines both humorous and tense?

You should write about:

- what happens to create humour and tension
- the writer's use of language and structure to create humour and tension
- the effects on the reader. **(10 marks)**

Writing about language and structure

For a question like this you should:

- ✓ spend about 12 minutes on your answer
- ✓ read the question carefully and **highlight the main focus**
- ✓ only use the lines of the text **referred to in the question**
- ✓ identify the **language** and **structural devices** used and comment on their **effects.**

Sample answer extract

The writer uses direct speech to create humour when Will calls the bread 'a bloody french loaf'. Direct speech throughout the extract also shows the reader more about the characters and what Marcus feels about them. Marcus answers Will in short sentences, this suggests he is nervous or scared.

✓ Clear opening point with good use of a short quotation for supporting evidence

✗ Interesting point but no evidence or explanation of its effect is offered

✗ Good point with some explanation but does not address the focus of the question

Avoid making points that aren't supported by evidence or explained. Make sure the evidence you choose helps you to answer the main focus of the question.

Improved sample answer

The writer creates humour and tension by using a mixture of direct speech, reported thoughts and action. Will's speech creates humour when he calls the bread 'a bloody french loaf' but Marcus appears to be too worried to respond to this as he is later said to hate him 'even more'. Marcus also answers Will in short sentences, suggesting he is nervous or scared, which adds to the tension of the scene.

✓ Effective overview at start of answer

✓ Clear points address question and are developed by use of short, relevant quotes

✓ Good point fully developed with key focus of question clearly addressed

This answer is clearly focused on what the question asks. Always check that you do the same.

Now try this

Read the rest of the extract from *About a Boy*, from line 36 to the end. Complete the 'Improved sample answer' by identifying and commenting on **two** further structural devices.

Remember: it isn't enough just to identify a language or structural device. You also need to explain its effects. If you know it, use the technical name for a device, too.

Putting it into practice

In **Component 2: Section A – Reading**, you'll need to respond to the **language** and **structure** in **non-fiction** texts. Read the extract from *Who'd Be a Paper Boy?* on page 100. Then look at the exam-style question and read the extracts from two students' answers.

Worked example

A2 John Crace is trying to argue that modern teenagers are unwilling to earn their money. How does he try to do this?

You should comment on:
- what he says to influence readers
- his use of language and structure
- the way he presents his argument. **(10 marks)**

Writing about language and structure

For a question like this you should:
- ✓ spend about 12 minutes on your answer
- ✓ read the question carefully and **highlight the main focus**
- ✓ identify the **language** and **structural devices** used and comment on their **effects**.

Sample answer extract

The writer starts with a list of three to emphasise the negative aspects of doing a paper round. This is followed by alliteration 'insult to injury' which creates humour as most readers will not feel that doing a paper round before school is very hard work.

After giving his opinion that in the past teenagers were happy to do this job, the writer then uses an expert opinion from a shop owner. The shop owner uses statistics, which makes her seem truthful.

✗ A clear point and identification of technique but no comment on effect

✓ A clear point, identification of technique and explanation

✗ Identification of techniques and clear reference to the extract, but no developed explanation of how this helps writer's argument

Improved sample answer

The writer uses a mixture of hyperbolic humorous opinions and statistics to argue that teenagers are too lazy to bother earning money. Starting with a list of three negative aspects of doing a paper round and then using the alliterative phrase 'insult to injury' creates humour as most readers will not feel that doing a paper round before school is hard work.

After giving his opinion that in the past teenagers were happy to do this job, the writer then provides expert evidence from a shop owner. The use of statistics from this expert, like '£20', provides concrete evidence that will persuade most adult readers that teenagers are lazy, as it seems like a lot of money for just 18 deliveries.

✓ Clear overview that addresses question and identifies main argument used in article

✓ Clearly addresses both structure ('list of three') and language ('alliterative phrase') and uses the technical names for the devices

✓ A fully developed explanation

Notice how this well-structured answer focuses tightly on the 'how' in the question.

Now try this

Continue with the 'Improved sample answer' on *Who'd Be a Paper Boy?* opposite. You are aiming to identify at least **three** more points from lines 25–54 in the extract.

Handling two texts

In **Component 2: Section A – Reading** you will have two questions that ask you to refer to **both** of the non-fiction texts in your answer. The texts will always be linked by a **common theme or topic** so will always have something in common. You will need to write about the **similarities** and **differences**. The questions on this page are sample questions and do not need to be answered.

To answer the following questions you will need to use both texts.

A5 According to these two writers, what are the hardships of foreign travel? **(4 marks)**

Look at the marks available. This synthesis question is only worth 4 marks, so you only need to take an overview and back this up with two or three points.

Similarities and differences

The texts may be similar or different in various ways, for example in terms of:

- the ideas they express about the topic
- the perspective (point of view) they take about the topic
- the language they use
- the way they are structured.

Question A5

The first of these two questions will ask you to **select information** from the two non-fiction texts and show your understanding by writing about them together. This is often referred to as **synthesis**.

synthesise *verb*
To combine (a number of things) into a coherent whole.
Synonyms: combine, fuse, amalgamate, build a whole.

Turn to pages 35 and 36 to find out more about synthesising evidence

You will need to:

1. take an overview
2. back your overview up with two or three relevant points
3. show a clear understanding of both texts.

A6 Both of these texts are about foreign travel. Compare the following:
- the writers' attitudes to travel
- how they get across their points about travel. **(10 marks)**

This question carries 10 marks, so spend some time revising how to compare effectively. You will need to compare the writers' ideas, as well as the actual language used.

Question A6

The second question will ask you to **compare** two non-fiction texts.

compare *verb*
To examine (two or more objects, ideas, people, etc.) in order to note similarities and differences.

See pages 38–41 for more about comparing texts

You will need to:

1. compare the writers' ideas and views
2. compare how the writers present these ideas and views
3. give examples from the text and use them in a detailed comparison.

Now try this

1 Which of the two questions that use both texts (A5 or A6) should you spend the most time answering?
2 How many points do you need to make when answering the synthesis question (A5)?
3 Which question requires you to look in detail at the language used in the texts?

Selecting evidence for synthesis

Question A5 in **Component 2: Section A – Reading** asks you to select information from two non-fiction texts and **write about both texts together**. This can be challenging and the first step is to **select evidence** that is relevant to the question.

To answer the following question you will need to use both texts.

A5 According to these two writers, what are the hardships of foreign travel? **(4 marks)**

Highlight key words in the question before you start your answer. This will help you select relevant information and keep your answer focused.

To revise skim reading, see page 6

Selecting relevant information

For this type of question, you need to select **evidence that is relevant to the question**.

1. **Skim read** the longer text to find the main idea of each paragraph.
2. Aim to pick out **two pieces of evidence** that are relevant to the question.
3. Then **skim read** the second text.
4. Find **two pieces of evidence** that you can combine – or **synthesise** – with the evidence from the first text.

Remember to look at sentence types when thinking about structure, and always look carefully at the beginning and end of the text to spot changes in tone.

First text

Here are two pieces of evidence you might select from *The Hungry Cyclist*.

Extracts from The Hungry Cyclist. *Full text on page 104. Lines 1–3.*

The air was cold and thin. Gasping for breath I said goodbye to a country I had fallen in love with and entered another.

Lines 6–7.

Gone were the smiles and friendly cheers of encouragement from the roadside. Gone were the picturesque colonial farmsteads with their flower-covered porches…

Point 1: The new country is harsh and the writer almost feels unwell when he arrives.

Point 2: The people and the landscape he sees are unwelcoming.

Skim reading the rest of the article shows that the writer adds more about point 2 above, and then starts to enjoy his time in Ecuador. So the second part of the article may not be relevant to the focus of the question.

Second text

Here are two pieces of evidence you might select from *Letters from Sydney*:

Point 1: country also harsh, with dense forest

Point 2: encounters unfamiliar people so it seems unwelcoming

Extracts from Letters from Sydney. *Full text on page 105. Lines 15–16.*

… part of which was a dense forest, 160 miles through…

Lines 17–18.

… now and then a black fellow and his family to be seen, stark naked, and about every 50 or 70 miles, a lonely shepherd gunya…

Now try this

Read the rest of the extracts from *The Hungry Cyclist* and *Letters from Sydney* and find **one** further similarity that could be synthesised to answer the question above.

Had a look ☐ Nearly there ☐ Nailed it! ☐

Synthesising evidence

Once you have selected the evidence you need to respond to **Question A5** in **Component 2: Section A – Reading**, you need to **synthesise** the points in your answer.

Structuring your synthesis

To **synthesise the evidence** you have selected:

1. Start with an overview that sums up the main points of your answer.

Make sure your overview includes key words from the question.

2. Write **one sentence for each piece of evidence** you selected.
3. Use **adverbials** to signpost the way through your synthesis.

Linking ideas

Use adverbials and linking phrases like these in your synthesis to show the similarity between the pieces of evidence:

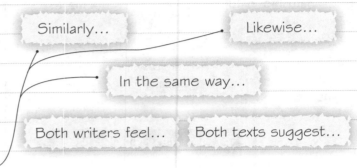

Similarly…

Likewise…

In the same way…

Both writers feel…

Both texts suggest…

Look back at page 35 for a reminder about selecting evidence for synthesis

Worked example

To answer the following question you will need to use both texts.

A5 According to these two writers, what are the hardships of foreign travel? **(4 marks)**

For both writers the hardships of foreign travel were that they found the new countries they visited to be harsh and unwelcoming. Both writers found the landscape and countryside was harsh: in Ecuador the air was 'cold and thin' and in Sydney the forest was 'dense'. Likewise they did not feel welcomed, as in Australia the people were unfamiliar to the writer and in Ecuador the people did not smile when the writer cycled past.

The overview uses key words from the question which clearly signal that the answer will be relevant.

Clearly signals that the answer is synthesising evidence from both texts.

These are the pieces of evidence the student selected:

Extract from The Hungry Cyclist. *Full text on page 104. Lines 1–7.*

The air was cold and thin. Gasping for breath I said goodbye to a country I had fallen in love with and entered another.

Gone were the smiles and friendly cheers of encouragement from the roadside. Gone were the picturesque colonial farmsteads with their flower-covered porches…

Extract from Letters from Sydney. *Full text on page 105. Lines 15–18.*

… part of which was a dense forest, 160 miles through…

… now and then a black fellow and his family to be seen, stark naked, and about every 50 or 70 miles, a lonely shepherd gunya…

Now try this

Write **one** more synthesis paragraph about *The Hungry Cyclist* (full text on page 104) and *Letters from Sydney* (full text on page 105). You could use the point you selected on page 35 in your answer.

Remember to stick closely to the main focus of Question A5 above.

Looking closely at language

Question A6 in **Component 2: Section A – Reading** asks you to look closely at both the **language** and the **structure** in **two non-fiction texts** and **compare** the **effects** that are created.

Analysing the texts

Before you can answer the comparison question you need to look very closely at the texts and question the language and structure the writer has chosen to use. You could ask yourself:

To revise rhetorical devices, turn to pages 25 and 26

What rhetorical devices has the writer chosen to use? What effect do they have?

Turn to pages 28 and 29 for a reminder about sentence structure

What types and lengths of sentences has the writer used? What effect do they have?

Use of a list and pattern of three to emphasise how inadequate and nervous he was on his first day.

Short sentence contrasts with the long sentences that deliver the anecdote in the opening paragraph and changes tone of article to one that is more serious.

Extract from The History of London's Black Cabs. *Full text on page 102. Lines 1–8.*

When I picked up my first fare in Covent Garden last month, I couldn't even open the passenger doors. I had two gentlemen fresh from dinner in Langley Street, and I was panicking, pressing all the buttons I could find, fumbling with keys. Nonetheless they were delighted when I told them they were my first, and that consequently the ride – as goes the cabbie tradition – was free, to wherever they wanted to go. Clapham Junction, as it happened, though they might as well have said Tuxedo Junction as far as my frayed nerves were concerned.

When I started learning the Knowledge of London in October 2008, the examiner told us it was the hardest thing we would ever do. He wasn't exaggerating.

Build-up of negative verbs with connotations of nervous struggle; 'frayed' suggests he is literally falling apart under the pressure.

Opens with an anecdote to elicit the reader's empathy and establish the writer's knowledge about the topic.

What connotations are created by the language the writer has chosen? What tone does the language create?

Find out more about connotations on page 18

What structure has the writer used? How do the opening and conclusion of the text differ? What effect does this have?

To revise the structure of non-fiction texts, see page 30

Now try this

Turn to page 14 to refresh your P-E-E skills

Look at the second paragraph (lines 7–18) from *The History of London's Black Cabs*. Identify **two** further points you could make about language and/or structure. Write a P-E-E paragraph about each point, supporting your points with evidence from the text and commenting on its effect.

Planning to compare

In **Component 2: Section A – Reading**, the comparison question **(Question A6)** is the most challenging. In this question, you will be asked to **compare two non-fiction texts**. It is important to set aside a couple of minutes for **planning** before you start writing.

Worked example

To answer the following question you will need to use both texts.

A6 Both of these texts are about children working. Compare the following:

- the writers' attitudes to children working
- how they get across their arguments. **(10 marks)**

You must use the text to support your comments and make it clear which text you are referring to.

Approaches to comparing

When comparing two texts you could:

- identify similar language or structural techniques in both texts and then explain the effects they create OR
- find similar effects (such as tone or ideas) and explain the different techniques the writers have used to achieve these effects.

Look at one student's planning and an extract from their answer below.

Extract from Who'd Be a Paper Boy? *Full text on page 100. Lines 1–11.*

It's cold, it's dark and you've got to bolt your breakfast before dragging a bag full of papers round the streets. To add insult to injury, you then have to go to school. So who would be bothered with a paper round? Almost no one these days, it seems.

Twenty years ago, a paper round was one of the few ways for a teenager to earn a few quid to squander on a packet of No 6 and a bottle of cider, and the kids who did it generally took it seriously.

- Pattern of three at start to show negative side of paper rounds.
- Alliteration for humour.
- Rhetorical question to involve audience.
- Colloquial language for emphasis.

Extract from Victorian Child Labour. *Full text on page 101. Line 1–4.*

The other is the old, the often-repeated, and as often-refuted, argument that the work is light. Light! Why, no doubt, much of it is light, if measured by the endurance of some three or four minutes. But what say you, my Lords, to a continuity of toil, in a standing posture, in a poisonous atmosphere, during 13 hours, with 15 minutes of rest?

- Pattern of three and repetition instantly engages the audience.
- Rhetorical question also engages.
- Factual numbers for emphasis.
- Emotive language for emphasis.

Sample answer

Both writers use rhetorical questions to engage and challenge their audience. However, in *Who'd Be a Paper Boy?*, the question is used to sum up the humorous comments the writer has made, whereas in *Victorian Child Labour* the question is far more serious. This writer uses emotive language such as 'toil' and 'poisonous', which are intended to emphasise the awful nature of child labour.

- Highlights a similarity between the texts
- Signals that there are also differences
- Evidence and explanation of how one of the texts gets across its point and reveals the writer's attitude, picking up on key points in the question

Now try this

Using the student's planning notes about language above, write **one** additional paragraph in answer to the exam-style question. Use P-E-E to structure your paragraph and remember to refer to both texts.

Comparing ideas

When **comparing** texts in **Component 2**, you will also need to write about the writers' **ideas**. You will need to use the **language comparison skills** that are covered on pages 37 and 38 in order to do this.

To answer the following question you will need to use both texts.

A6 Both of these texts are about children working.

Compare the following:

- the writers' attitudes to children working
- how they get across their arguments. **(10 marks)**

You must use the text to support your comments and make it clear which text you are referring to.

You need to analyse the language and structure used by each writer and use your findings to compare how the writers present their ideas.

You need to use quotations.

Comparing ideas

1. Start with the longer text and skim read it to find the main idea of each paragraph.
2. Use your 'planning to compare' skills to find language and structure points you can use to explain how the main ideas are presented.
3. Do the same for the shorter text.
4. In your comparison, make it clear which text you are referring to at any time by using the name of the writer (e.g. 'Crace suggests...') or the form of the text (e.g. 'The speech shows...').

Extract from Who'd Be a Paper Boy? *Full text on page 100. Line 25–33.*

You can have some sympathy for the kids. Standards in literacy and numeracy have fallen so steeply that it can be a real struggle identifying door names and numbers, and the Sunday papers are now so heavy that your averagely obese teenager just doesn't have the strength or stamina for the job. But the bottom line is that most kids can no longer be bothered to get out of bed for £20.

Extract from Victorian Child Labour. *Full text on page 101. Line 9–13.*

I asked for a collection of cripples and deformities. In a short time more than 80 were gathered in a large courtyard. They were mere samples of the entire mass. I assert without exaggeration that no power of language could describe the varieties, and I may say, the cruelties, in all these degradations of the human form. They stood or squatted before me in all the shapes of the letters of the alphabet.

Similarity in main idea: both texts deal with the physical side of children working.

By 'main idea' we mean the main topic of the texts.

Similarity in language: both writers use exaggeration (**hyperbole**) to reinforce their point.

Difference in language and effect: Crace's hyperbole has a sarcastic tone, reinforcing his suggestion that teenagers are either physically or academically unable to work, whereas Hansard uses emotive language to emphasise the terrible deformities caused by child labour.

Now try this

Look at the extracts from *Who'd Be a Paper Boy?* and *Victorian Child Labour*. Find one piece of evidence in **each** text to back up the following point which highlights a **difference** in the writers' ideas: Crace feels that teenagers undertake relatively light work, whereas the Hansard speech states that the work in 1838 was extremely harsh for children.

Had a look ☐ Nearly there ☐ Nailed it! ☐

Comparing perspective

When **comparing texts** in **Component 2**, you will also need to write about the **perspective** of each writer.

perspective *noun*
A particular attitude towards or way of regarding something; a point of view.
Synonyms: outlook, attitude, view, position, stand, feelings about an idea.

Identifying perspectives

Both texts in **Component 2** will cover a similar topic. As you are skim reading for the main idea, make sure you identify how both writers feel about the topic. Writers often make their perspective clear at the start of their text, or sometimes at the start of the second paragraph. Here is an example of how to identify perspective:

Extract from A History of London's Black Cabs. *Full text on page 102. Lines 1–3.*

When I picked up my first fare in Covent Garden last month, I couldn't even open the passenger doors. I had two gentlemen fresh from dinner in Langley Street, and I was panicking, pressing all the buttons I could find, fumbling with keys.

This opening paragraph makes it clear that the writer found life as a cab driver difficult – he 'couldn't even open the passenger doors'.

Extract from Victorian Cab Drivers. *Full text on page 103. Lines 10–11.*

When I go and look at them after breakfast, it appears to me that the cabman's lot in life is not an unhappy one.

This second paragraph suggests the writer's perspective is that being a cab driver is quite pleasant – 'not an unhappy one' – and probably quite easy.

The words 'feels' and 'suggestion' show understanding of the writers' perspectives.

An overview is used to introduce the comparison of perspectives.

Clear signpost introduces further detail.

Initially, the writer of *Victorian Cab Drivers* feels that the life of a cab driver is rather pleasant, whereas the suggestion in *The History of London's Black Cabs* is that being a cab driver is difficult. To show this, the writer uses...

Note how this answer discusses perspectives and makes a comparison in the same sentence.

Now try this

Read the extracts from *The History of London's Black Cabs* and *Victorian Cab Drivers*. Do the writers keep the same perspective throughout or do they end with a different point of view?

Remember, you will need to write about structure, too, so looking at differences between the beginning and end of texts is a good idea when thinking about perspective.

For a reminder about structure in non-fiction texts, see page 30

Answering a compare question

Writing about and **comparing two texts** for **Component 2** is difficult. To make your answer clear to an examiner and to fully show your understanding, you need to use an effective structure for your answer.

Structure

Aim to make direct comparisons.

You could **focus on one language feature** or its effect in the first text, then compare it to a similar feature or effect in the second text.

You could also **explore differences** – for example, writing about the different tones of the two texts and how language is used to achieve them.

Linking words and phrases

Use adverbials to signpost the way through your answer.

For example, you could **signpost a similarity** using adverbials like: 'Similarly...' or 'In the same way...'

To **signpost a difference** you can use adverbials like: 'However...' or 'On the other hand...'

Worked example

Write a brief overview in one sentence summarising the two texts and their purposes.

Both texts are about... but Text 1 aims to... while Text 2 tries to...

Write about a language feature in **Text 1**, supported with evidence and an explanation of its effect on the reader.

Text 1 uses...

Similarly, Text 2 uses...

Use an adverbial to link a point about a similar language feature in **Text 2**. Support this with evidence and explanation as well.

Both texts use emotive language. For example, Text 1...

This makes the reader realise that...

On the other hand, Text 2 uses emotive language to achieve a different effect...

The writer has created a humorous tone in Text 1. He has done this by using puns such as...

However, the writer of Text 2 has created a much more disturbing tone by...

Getting it right

Remember that you can write about a difference in the two texts – for example, a similar language feature which has a different effect in the two texts. You can also write about how the writers have used language to support their different purposes, appealed to different audiences or created different ideas and perspectives.

Remember to skim read the texts first, noting down how the main ideas are presented. It will then be easier to find points of comparison. Don't forget to be clear which text you are referring to.

Now try this

Read *Who'd Be a Paper Boy?* and *Victorian Child Labour* (full texts on pages 100 and 101). Use the structure in the 'Worked example' above to write the **first paragraph** of an answer to Question A6 on page 39.

Try to use the words 'idea' and 'perspective' in your answer. Remember to spend a couple of minutes planning before you start to write.

Had a look ☐ Nearly there ☐ Nailed it! ☐

Putting it into practice

In **Component 2: Section A – Reading** you will need to **compare** the writers' **ideas and perspectives**, and how they are presented, in **two non-fiction texts**. Read the extracts from *The History of London's Black Cabs* on page 102 and *Victorian Cab Drivers* on page 103. Then look at the exam-style question below and read the extracts from two students' answers.

Worked example

To answer the following question you will need to use both texts.

A6 Both of these texts are about cab driving in London.

Compare the following:

- the writers' attitudes to the occupation of cab driving
- how they get across their ideas and arguments. **(10 marks)**

You must use the text to support your comments and make it clear which text you are referring to.

Comparing writers' ideas and perspectives

For a question like this you should:

- ✓ spend about 12 minutes on your answer
- ✓ read the question carefully and **highlight the main focus**
- ✓ spend a couple of minutes **planning** your answer before you start writing
- ✓ identify the **language** and **structural devices** used and comment on how they help the writer to get across their **ideas** and **arguments**.

Sample answer extract

Beetlestone's article is about him being a cab driver and the Victorian text is about a man watching cab drivers. Beetlestone starts with an anecdote about his first day which shows straight away that he found the job difficult, for instance he was 'panicking' and 'fumbling'. The Victorian text opens with a personal note about him being 'confined to the house' and then he gives his point of view about cab driving, which is that he thinks it provides a 'not unhappy' life.

✗ Some comment about the main idea, but no overview or comparison given

✓ Examples of language device and structure ('starts with'), with some explanation of their effect

✗ Identification of structure ('opens with') but no comment on how this helps the writer get his ideas across

✓ Clear identification of perspective with relevant evidence

Note how this well-structured answer focuses on the key points in the question (the writers' attitudes and **how** their ideas are presented) and how each sentence refers to **both** texts.

Improved sample answer

Both texts are about cab driving in London but while Beetlestone argues that it is a difficult job, the Victorian writer's perspective is that life as a cab driver is very pleasant. Both texts start on a personal note, Beetlestone with an anecdote about his difficult first day and the Victorian text with a story about how he spends his afternoons. However, Beetlestone does this to emphasise from the beginning that the job is difficult even after training, whereas the Victorian writer does it to show how restful the life of cab drivers appears to be.

✓ Clear overview comparing the main idea and the perspectives of the writers

✓ Identifies a similarity in language

✓ Identifies a difference in effect

✓ Fully developed explanation of effects

Now try this

Complete the 'Improved sample answer' on *The History of London's Black Cabs* and *Victorian Cab Drivers* opposite with **at least one** more paragraph. Try to pick up on both similarities and differences in the language and structure.

Evaluating a text: fiction

Both components will have a question that tests your ability to **evaluate** texts. In **Component 1** you will need to evaluate a **fiction** text.

evaluate *verb*
To assess something and form an idea about its value
Synonyms: form an opinion of, make up one's mind about, get the measure of, weigh up, analyse

Approaching evaluation

Read the question → Skim read the text → Read the text in detail → Write your answer

- Read the question: This will tell you what aspects of the text to evaluate
- Skim read the text: What are your impressions?
- Read the text in detail: Form an opinion and identify evidence to back it up
- Write your answer: Use inference to explain and assess the effects of the text

Understanding an evaluation question

A5 The first twenty or so lines of this extract encourage the reader to view the narrator's father as a good man.
To what extent do you agree with this view?
You should write about:
- your own impressions of the father as he is presented here and in the extract as a whole
- how the writer has created these impressions. **(10 marks)**

You need to focus on specific lines of the extract as well as referring to the extract as a whole.

Keep focused on the key words in the question that tell you what to look for – here the focus is on the narrator's father, not the narrator.

This means you need to use evidence from the text and explain how the writer has used language and structure for effect.

This means you need to consider both sides of the argument – what in the text supports this view and what doesn't.

Responding to an evaluation question

Keep the focus of the question in mind as you read the text and identify evidence that supports either side of the argument.

Extract from My Son's Story. *Full text on page 98. Lines 1–4.*

We didn't have any particular sense of what we were – my sister and I. I mean, my father made of the circumscription of our life within the areas open to us a charmed circle. Of a kind. I see that I don't want to admit that, now, because it comes to me as a criticism, but the truth is that it did give us some sort of security.

Father kept harsh reality of life under apartheid ('circumscription') from children, so appears to be a good man – supports view in question.

Father managed to create happy childhood ('charmed circle') for them despite restrictions – supports view in question.

Suggestion that while he gave them 'some sort of security', he should have been more honest about the realities of apartheid, so perhaps did have some faults – looks at the other side of the argument.

Remember, you need to focus on the extract but look at the whole text, too. This will help show you understand any changes in tone or the way a character is presented.

Now try this

Read lines 1–14 of the extract from *My Son's Story* and make **two** more inferences about the father that you could use to answer **Question A5** above.

You should use quotations to back up your points but there is no need to analyse language or structure in detail for this type of question. For example, you might observe 'their childhood is happy, a "charmed circle" created by their father' but you do not need to go on to discuss the connotations of the word 'charmed'.

Evaluating a text: non-fiction

Both components will have a question that tests your ability to **evaluate** texts. In **Component 2** you will need to evaluate a **non-fiction** text.

Evaluating non-fiction

Read the extract.

A4 What do you think and feel about the writer's experience of Australia?

You should comment on:

- what is said
- how it is said. **(10 marks)**

You must refer to the text to support your comments.

The wording here is different from that in an evaluation question for fiction. It still means you need to use inference to assess the text, and evidence to back up your views.

Getting it right

Remember to:

- read the **question** carefully and pick out the **key words**
- refer to the **whole text** – no specific line numbers are given
- **skim read** and then read the text in more **detail**, forming your **opinions** and **identifying evidence**
- use your **inference** skills to **explain** and **assess** the text.

Extract from Letters from Sydney. *Full text on page 105. Lines 2–7.*

This comes with my kind love to you both, as also to my brothers and sisters and I hope you will excuse me for not writing before, as I have been so put about. I arrived in Sydney on the 9th of June, after a fine, but long passage, since when I have worked at my trade but two months out of a year and ten months that I have been here. As many others are compelled to do, I was forced to go up the country, 850 miles from Sydney, as a shepherd, at the low wages of £15 per year.

Negative view from the beginning – conditions so bad he hasn't had time to write home

Suggests he came with high hopes ('fine, but long passage') – perhaps the long time at sea allowed him to build up unrealistic hopes

Feels Australia has treated him and others unfairly ('compelled' and 'forced')

His negative feelings may be a little unfair as at least he found work in Australia, even at low pay

Note how inference is used to evaluate here, and is backed up by evidence from the text.

Responding to an evaluation question

Keep the focus of the question in mind as you read the text and identify evidence that supports either side of the argument. Use key words and the bullet points in the question to keep your evaluation focused.

Now try this

Read the rest of the extract (lines 7–34) from *Letters from Sydney*. Identify **two** more points you could make to answer the evaluation question above.

Remember to:

- comment on what is said and how it is said
- look closely at the beginning and end of the extract – does the tone change, for example?

Turn to page 30 to revise structure in non-fiction

Using evidence to evaluate

For **both components**, you need to use carefully chosen, **relevant evidence** to support the **points** you make in your answers. Quotations can be long or short, but you must use them correctly in your answer to obtain maximum marks.

The writer uses a rhetorical question to sum up the key point of the speech:

'What say you, then, of children – children of the tenderest years?'

This question challenges the reader and makes it clear that the speaker feels horrified and angry about the age of children who are put to work.

Longer quotes: what to do

1. Introduce longer quotations with a colon.
2. Start the quotation on a new line.
3. Put your quotation in quotation marks.
4. Copy your quotation accurately.
5. Start your explanation on a new line.

Embedding quotations means you can include P-E-E in one sentence to save time!

The writer's use of emotive language like 'deformed' and 'crippled' suggests he feels very strongly about the harmful effects of child labour.

Shorter quotes: what to do

1. You do not need to introduce each quotation with a colon or start a new line.
2. Put each quotation into quotation marks.
3. Make sure the sentence containing the embedded quotation makes sense.
4. Choose single-word quotations very carefully to ensure you can make an effective comment on them.

Paraphrasing the text

Sometimes, as in the example below, you can refer closely to the text by turning it into your own words. This is called **paraphrasing**.

Remember, paraphrasing is effective when evaluating a text but you need to use short quotations when you answer questions on language.

Extract from Victorian Child Labour. *Full text on page 101. Lines 14–16.*

When I visited Bradford, under the limitation of hours some years afterwards, I called for a similar exhibition of cripples…

The writer perhaps feels extremely strongly about the effects of labour on young children as he witnessed them first hand in Bradford. He does seem very emotional about the issue and this is probably as he asked to see the affected children for himself.

Now try this

Look back at the annotations about the extract from *Letters from Sydney* on page 44. Use them to write **two** P-E-E paragraphs explaining what you think and feel about the writer's experience of Australia. Remember to comment on **what** is said and **how** it is said.

Only use one longer quotation per answer. It is often better to stick to shorter quotations as these show that you can identify key words and phrases.

Had a look ☐ Nearly there ☐ Nailed it! ☐

Putting it into practice

In **Component 1: Section A – Reading**, you'll need to **evaluate** a fiction text and **support** and **explain** your evaluation with evidence from the text. Read the extract from *About a Boy* on page 99. Then look at the exam-style question below and read the extracts from two students' answers.

Worked example

Read lines 1–11.

A5 'In the first twenty or so lines of this extract, the reader is encouraged to feel sympathy for Marcus.'

To what extent do you agree with this view?

You should write about:

- your own impressions of Marcus as he is presented here and in the extract as a whole
- how the writer has created these impressions. **(10 marks)**

Evaluating fiction

For a question like this you should:

- ✓ spend about 12 minutes on your answer
- ✓ read the question carefully and **highlight the main focus**
- ✓ only use the lines of the text **referred to in the question**
- ✓ use **inference** and **evidence from the text** to **explain** your ideas and assess the **effect** of the text.

Sample answer

Marcus is shown to be a pessimist in these lines. The writer repeats the idea of 'trying' three times to suggest that he does not believe in his abilities. This might make a reader feel sympathy for him. Marcus also tries to excuse his poor behaviour by calling the duck 'pathetic' and this makes me like him less.

✓ Clear point, supported by evidence and an explanation

✓ Good focus on question, using key words from the question

✗ A personal response to the character but lacks a clear explanation

Note how this answer focuses on the question and begins to look at both sides of the argument with the final point about excuses.

Improved sample answer

Overall, the reader is encouraged to feel some sympathy for Marcus as he is presented as a boy who does not succeed despite trying hard. The writer repeats the idea of 'trying' three times to suggest that he does not believe in his abilities. This might make a reader feel sympathy for him. However, the writer's use of an interior monologue also shows Marcus as a boy who tries to justify his poor behaviour; he calls the duck 'pathetic'. Readers might not be as sympathetic at this point as he is presented as not facing up to the consequences of his behaviour.

✓ Clear overview at the start of the answer which uses key words from the question

✓ 'However' clearly signals that an alternative point of view is being considered

✓ Clear use of evidence with explanations that refer back to the question

Remember that not all your points have to agree with the statement in the question. 'Evaluate' means to 'weigh up' and then judge. Better answers will consider alternative points of view.

Now try this

Complete the 'Improved sample answer' on *About a Boy* opposite with **one** further evaluative point.

Putting it into practice

In **Component 2: Section A – Reading**, you'll need to **evaluate** a non-fiction text and **support** and **explain** your evaluation with evidence from the text. Read the extract from *Victorian Child Labour* on page 101. Then look at the exam-style question below and read the extracts from two students' answers.

Worked example

A4 What do you think and feel about the writer's views about child labour?

You should comment on:
- what is said
- how it is said. **(10 marks)**

You must refer to the text to support your comments.

Evaluating non-fiction

For a question like this you should:
- ✓ spend about 12 minutes on your answer
- ✓ read the question carefully and **highlight the main focus**
- ✓ refer to the **whole text** unless specific line numbers are given in the question
- ✓ use **inference** and **evidence from the text** to **explain** your ideas and assess the **effect** of the text.

Sample answer

I think that the writer shows a lot of sympathy for the children working in factories. The phrase 'stunted, crippled, deformed, useless' shows that the writer feels very strongly about how harmful the labour is. The fact that he speaks from personal experience 'what I have seen' makes it more persuasive.

✓ Some attempt to provide an overview.

✗ Clear evidence and explanation, but this is not from the opening of the text so does not signal full understanding of the text as a whole.

✗ A good point, but the explanation is not fully developed.

Older texts sometimes express ideas and views that differ from those held by most people today. Be careful not to dismiss them simply as 'old-fashioned'.

The form (a speech) will affect the way a writer expresses their views and will have an effect on the response of the reader.

Improved sample answer

Opening paragraph of answer:

The writer expresses very passionate views about the use of child labour. He seems to exaggerate with repetition of the word 'light' at the start, followed by the hyperbolic statement that they work in a 'poisonous atmosphere'. However, the extract is from a speech to parliament and his views would therefore be expected to be expressed in a very persuasive manner.

Final paragraph of answer:

Modern readers might find the writer's final point about praising God for the lack of 'cripples' disturbing as it suggests that he still accepts that very young children should work. However, the fact that he needs to raise the issue in parliament shows that his campaigning views may have been unusual at the time.

✓ Good overview that shows a clear focus on the question.

✓ Relevant evidence from the opening and slightly later in the text shows understanding of the whole extract.

✓ Clear explanation which evaluates the reason for the writer's use of hyperbole.

✓ Clear evaluation which takes into account different views in 21st century.

Now try this

Write the middle paragraph of the 'Improved sample answer' on *Victorian Child Labour* opposite.

Had a look ☐ Nearly there ☐ Nailed it! ☐

Writing questions: an overview

Both components of the English Language GCSE include a **Writing** section (Section B). There are different types of writing task in each component.

For a reminder about how the English Language GCSE is structured, turn to page 1

Component 1: Section B – Writing

Component 1: Section B – Writing → Creative Prose Writing → Write one text from a choice of four titles

Component 1 tests your ability to write **imaginatively** and **creatively**.

Component 2: Section B – Writing

Component 2: Section B – Writing

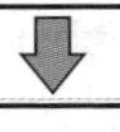

Transactional/ Persuasive Writing → Answer **two** questions. The topic of the first question will be the same as the text given in Component 2: Section A – Reading

Component 2 tests your ability to write for **different audiences and purposes**.

Assessment objectives

Assessment objectives are the **skills** you are tested on in the exam questions. For Writing, the assessment objectives are the same for both components.

You need to remember what skills you will be tested on for each component. The exam papers will not remind you.

Assessment objective 5 tests your ability to:

- communicate clearly, effectively, and imaginatively, selecting and adapting tone, style and register for different forms, purposes and audiences

Select the right form for your writing and use the most appropriate language for your audience.

- organise information and ideas, using structural and grammatical features to support coherence and cohesion of texts.

Use sentences and paragraphs to organise and structure your writing so the meaning is clear.

Assessment objective 6 tests your ability to use a range of vocabulary and sentence structures for clarity, purpose and effect, with accurate spelling and punctuation.

You need to:

- vary the length and types of sentence you use
- spell and punctuate correctly
- use interesting and effective words.

Now try this

Answer the following questions using the information on this page.

- The questions in one component require you to use language that is appropriate for a specific audience. Which component is this?
- How many questions do you need to answer for **Component 2**?
- How many titles should you choose to respond to for **Component 1**?

Writing questions: Component 1

Component 1: Section B – Writing will test the quality of your **creative prose writing** skills. The questions on this page are sample questions and do not need to be answered.

Planning your time

It is important to plan and use your time in the exam carefully. Every minute counts!

Your Component 1 exam is 1 hour and 45 minutes long.

For **Section B – Writing**, you should spend:

- 10 minutes planning
- 35 minutes writing.

Planning your answer

It is worth spending some time **planning** your writing before your start. The more you plan, the less time you will waste when you are actually writing. The exam paper suggests you spend **10 minutes planning** the writing task.

The exam paper also tells you that you should write **between 450 and 600 words**. Keep this in mind when you are making your plan.

Reading the question

It is important to read the question carefully.

Choose **one** of the following titles for your writing:

Either, *(a)* Taking a Stand.

Or, *(b)* The Change.

Or, *(c)* Write about a time when you helped somebody in trouble.

Or, *(d)* Write a story which begins: I never thought I would be seen as a hero... **(40 marks)**

You must write a narrative (story) or a recount (structured account of a personal experience) for **Component 1**. You cannot write a poem or a play, and you cannot write a description unless it is part of a narrative or recount. If you write a recount, remember that it does not need to be a true, real-life event.

These titles do not tell you which form to use but you must write either a narrative or a recount.

This title tells you which form to use: you must write your answer as a narrative.

What is 'prose'?

This is an example of prose. Prose is continuous, paragraphed writing and is the form often used for narratives and recounts.

Extract from Rebecca. *Full text on page 96. Lines 1–2.*

Last night I dreamt I went to Manderley again. It seemed to me I stood by the iron gate leading to the drive, and for a while I could not enter, for the way was barred to me…

How the marks work

In **Component 1: Section B – Writing**, there are **40 marks** available.
They are awarded like this:

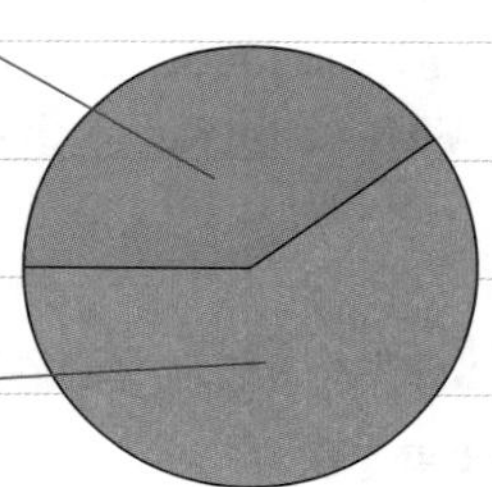

See page 48 for more detail on the assessment objectives for writing

Now try this

Choose **one** of the titles from the exam-style question above. Write the title as a heading and then spend 5 minutes jotting down as many ideas as you can, in the form of a spider diagram, for example.

Remember that in the exam you will need to spend a further 5 minutes organising your ideas into an effective structure.

For more about planning and structuring narrative, see pages 61 and 62

Writing questions: Component 2

Component 2: Section B – Writing will test the quality of your skills in **transactional** or **persuasive writing**. You need to show you can write effectively for **different audiences and purposes**. The questions on this page are sample questions and do not need to be answered.

Planning your time

For **Component 2** you must answer two writing questions.

Total time for Component 2 is 2 hours

For **Section B – Writing**, you should spend **30 minutes** on **each question**.

You could organise your time like this:

Question B1	Question B2
Plan: 5 minutes **Write:** 20 minutes **Check:** 5 minutes	**Plan:** 5 minutes **Write:** 20 minutes **Check:** 5 minutes

Taking time to plan each answer will help you to spend an equal amount of time actually writing each answer. **Both** questions in **Component 2** carry the **same marks**, so they both need the same planning and checking time. You will need to write between **300 and 400 words** for **each** answer.

Understanding the questions

B1 Your school/college is keen to encourage students to undertake voluntary work for the local community.

Write a report for the Headteacher suggesting ways to encourage students.

You could include:

- examples of types of voluntary work that would appeal to students
- reasons why students would benefit from voluntary work. **(20 marks)**

B2 Your school is considering shortening the summer holidays to just two weeks.

You have decided to write to the Headteacher to give your views on this proposal. You could write in favour or against the proposal.

Write a letter to the Headteacher giving your views. (20 marks)

Remember that you must answer **both questions**. In Component 2, you need to write between 300 and 400 words for each answer.

Take time to read the questions carefully. They will tell you what form to use and what audience to write for.

What is 'transactional writing'?

This type of writing is usually formal and is likely to be in the form of a letter, a report, an article or a speech.

transactional writing *noun*
Writing to get things done, to inform or persuade a particular audience to understand or do something

How the marks work

In **Component 2: Section B – Writing**, there are **40 marks** available. They are awarded like this:

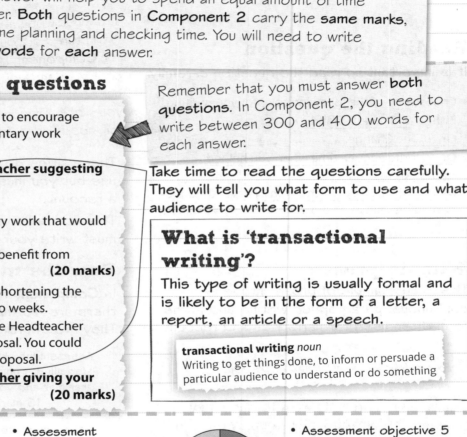

- Assessment objective 5 (communication) – 12 marks
- Assessment objective 6 (spelling, punctuation, grammar and vocabulary) – 8 marks

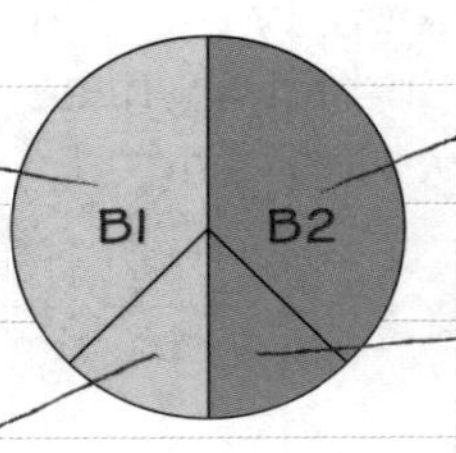

- Assessment objective 5 (communication) – 12 marks
- Assessment objective 6 (spelling, punctuation, grammar and vocabulary) – 8 marks

See page 48 for more detail on the assessment objectives for writing

Now try this

Write the title for the exam-style question B1 above as a heading and spend 5 minutes noting down as many ideas as you can. Then do the same for question B2. How would you need to structure your ideas to fit the form you are being asked to write in?

For more about ideas and planning, turn to pages 65 and 66

Writing for a purpose: creative

The focus of **Component 1: Section B – Writing** is **creative prose writing**. There are several techniques you can use to develop your ideas and engage the reader.

The five senses

I could feel the steady trickle of sweat across my forehead and down my temples, and as I stumbled over the cracked earth I was pursued by the furious buzzing of flies.

Use of the senses of touch ('feel') and sound ('buzzing') makes the description **vivid** and **engages** the reader.

When you describe a place or an experience, help the reader to imagine they are there – use the five senses of sight, sound, touch, taste and smell.

Many students only write about what can be seen. Use the other senses to help your writing stand out.

Figurative language

Used carefully and imaginatively, **figurative language**, or **imagery**, can create powerful pictures in the reader's mind. Figurative devices include:

- similes
- metaphors
- personification.

For a reminder about figurative devices, see page 19

Use your imagination! Similes like 'cool as a cucumber' and 'flat as a pancake' are not very original or creative.

Narrative voice and feelings

Unless the exam paper tells you which narrative voice to use, you can choose to write in the first or third person. Remember:

- a **first person narration** can give the reader **a sense of closeness to the narrator**
- You must stick to the narrative voice you choose throughout your answer!

Also see page 22 for a reminder about narrative voice

Describing the narrator's feelings can bring descriptive writing to life, too:

I smiled and felt very relaxed.

The reader is told the narrator feels relaxed but is not drawn into the scene.

A smile spread slowly across my lips and I felt all the tension drain from my limbs as I leant back into the chair and closed my eyes.

The verbs help the reader imagine the narrator's physical relaxation.

Language choice

The **quality** of your description is more important that the **quantity** of words you use. It is more effective to use fewer, but well-chosen words. For example:

This student answer creates a much more immediate image than the long sentence in the student answer below.

I danced across the road.

I walked cheerfully with a spring in my step across the road like I was dancing.

Avoid overloading your writing with figurative devices or descriptive techniques.

See page 75–79 for more about these techniques

Now try this

Remember to choose language for quality, not quantity. Try to use:

- at least two different senses
- verbs to show, rather than tell, how you felt
- at least one example of figurative language.

Write the **first paragraph** of your response to this **Component 1 creative prose writing** exam-style question.

Write about a time when you were desperately looking forward to an event. **(40 marks)**

Had a look ☐ Nearly there ☐ Nailed it! ☐

Writing for a purpose: inform, explain, review

For **Component 2: Section B – Writing** you will need to show you can write effectively for **different transactional purposes**. Transactional writing includes texts that **inform**, **explain or review**.

Also see pages 57–59 for more about form

Features to inform, explain and review

Headings and sub-headings
- especially useful for **information texts**
- use **headings** to organise the text
- use relevant **sub-headings** to make information easy to find

Facts and statistics

These suggest the information you are giving can be trusted.

If you are writing about the same topic as the reading texts in Section A, you could use facts and statistics from either or both of them. If not, you can make them up to suit the point you are making.

Be careful: the facts and statistics need to be believable!

Structure

Information and explanation texts:
- are usually **organised chronologically**
- have **time** or **temporal adverbials** which provide signposts:

First… Then… Next… Finally…

Reviews:
- usually start with a brief **summary**
- include the reviewer's **opinions**
- **avoid lengthy descriptions** of events.

Tone

Tone means the mood of a text, for example, serious, instructive, casual.
- Use a **formal tone** to suggest to the reader that the information is reliable.
- Use **standard English**.

Depending on your audience and topic, you could use humour – but take care not to overdo it!

Language

Texts that inform, explain or review are factual, so avoid using too much figurative language.

See page 19 for more about figurative devices

Getting it right

You can still use figurative language like similes and metaphors, but make sure the techniques you use support the purpose of the text. For example, if you are informing, explaining or reviewing, make sure you don't start describing!

Now try this

Look at this exam-style question and then complete the tasks below:

1 List **five** sub-headings you could use to organise your writing.

2 Write **one** sentence describing the tone you would use in this task.

3 Write down any facts or statistics you could include in your writing, for example the typical number of students in a class.

B1 Your school is starting a magazine to inform parents about school life.

Write an article for the first edition explaining what life is like for a Year 7 student at your school.

You could include:
- examples of what they will learn
- information about a typical day. **(20 marks)**

Writing for a purpose: argue and persuade

Transactional writing also includes texts that **argue** or **persuade**.

Also see pages 57–59 for more about form

Key points

The power of your argument or persuasion relies on the strength of your key points.

To argue:

> There are those who claim that modern teenagers are lazy and uncaring, yet nothing could be further from the truth. In fact, the numbers of teenagers actively involved in charitable causes is on the rise...

Choose points which highlight:

- why you are right
- why those who disagree are wrong.

To persuade:

> With the rise and rise of social media, it is hardly surprising that many teenagers today are comfortably cocooned in their own online oasis. What better way to coax them out into the daylight than to get them working with local charities...

Choose points which highlight:

- what is wrong with the way things are
- how your ideas will make things better.

Rhetorical devices

To engage your reader and add power to your argument or persuasive writing, use:

- rhetorical questions
- direct address
- repetition
- lists
- alliteration
- contrast
- pattern of three
- emotive language
- hyperbole.

Evidence

Always support **each** of your key points with convincing evidence. For example:

- facts or statistics
- an expert opinion
- an example from your own experience.

Linking ideas

Use adverbials to signpost the path your argument is going to follow.

To build your argument:

- furthermore...
- additionally/In addition...
- moreover...

To introduce counter-arguments:

- however...
- yet...
- on the other hand...

Also see page 71 for more about adverbials

To explain and develop your points:

- consequently/as a consequence...
- therefore...

Counter-arguments

Think about how your reader might disagree with you, and then point out why they are wrong. This is called making a 'counter-argument'. For example:

> Some people think that teenagers are lazy and uncaring. However, it is the media who give us these negative images...

Use adverbials to show that you are dismissing an opposing view.

Now try this

Look at this exam-style question and then complete the tasks.

1 Note down three key points you could use in your answer.
2 Make a counter-argument.
3 Write three sentences using two different rhetorical devices.

Choose your rhetorical devices with care and for impact. Avoid using too many rhetorical questions and patterns of three in particular.

B2 A proposal has been made by your local council to close the local sports centre and turn the building into a cinema.

You have decided to start a petition against this by writing to your local newspaper.

Write a letter to your local newspaper arguing that the sports centre should be kept open. (20 marks)

Had a look ☐ Nearly there ☐ Nailed it! ☐

Writing for an audience

For **Component 2: Section B – Writing** you will need to show you can write effectively for **different audiences.**

Identifying the audience

In some questions, the audience (person or people) you are writing for may be clearly **stated**:

> **B1** Write a letter for the Headteacher giving… **(20 marks)**

Your writing **must address** an adult (the Headteacher) and will require a formal response. As you are writing to a specific person, you could engage them directly by referring to their role – for example 'As a Headteacher, you will understand…'.

Other questions may only imply (hint at) an audience:

> **B2** … Write an engaging article for your local newspaper… **(20 marks)**

For this type of question you will need to think carefully about **who** would read this type of newspaper. In this case, it will probably be adults but may include teenagers.

Writing for an adult audience

When writing for an adult audience, you will usually need to write in a formal style and use standard English.

You should avoid non-standard English:

- texting language (e.g. LOL)
- slang (e.g. I was gutted)
- double negatives (e.g. I ain't never done that).

Worked example

> **B1** … Write an information guide for parents explaining how they can help their children with homework… **(20 marks)**

Parents can play a vital role in helping their children meet homework deadlines. Many teenagers, when a deadline has been missed, have a tendency to avoid dealing with the situation. Your role is to encourage them to speak to their teachers and ask for the help that is available at school.

Writing for a teenage audience

When writing for a teenage audience, or for younger children, you should still avoid non-standard English. However, some carefully used informal language may be an appropriate way to engage the audience.

Worked example

> **B1** … Write a speech for a Year 11 assembly persuading them that homework is a good idea. **(20 marks)**

Let's get things straight. Homework is a pain… and that's putting it mildly. We can all think of much better ways to occupy our time, and frequently many of us do just that! However, if you are behind with your homework, speak to your teacher as soon as you can. After all, they are there to help.

Notice how informal language has been carefully mixed with more formal language to engage the teenage audience.

Now try this

> **B1** … Write an article for your school website explaining why GCSE exams are important… **(20 marks)**

You reckon you've got ages until your GCSEs? You've already bagged a job? I'm telling you, those exams are coming round quick!

Rewrite the opening paragraph of this student answer, using formal standard English that is more appropriate to the audience.

Putting it into practice

In **Component 1: Section B – Writing**, you'll need to use your **creative writing skills** to write a piece of prose. Before you start writing, you should think carefully about the question.

How much time should you spend on planning and checking this question in your exam?

Timing	
Planning:	
Writing:	30 mins (10.10–10.40)
Checking:	

For a reminder about the structure of Component 1: Section B – Writing, go to page 49

Preparing for creative writing

You should:

- ✓ plan your time – you have **45 minutes** for this question, including planning and checking
- ✓ read the **question** carefully
- ✓ decide **which title** to answer
- ✓ **plan** your writing, including ideas about narrative voice and language techniques
- ✓ prepare to write **450 to 600 words.**

Look carefully at the exam-style question and the title options. Think about what each title might involve before you decide which one to answer. Look at one student's thoughts:

> Choose **one** of the following titles for your writing:
> **Either**, *(a)* The Feast.
> **Or**, *(b)* A Transformation.
> **Or**, *(c)* Write about your first day at school.
> **Or**, *(d)* Write a story which begins: Last night he had the dream again… **(40 marks)**

These two titles are fairly open and don't say which form to use. I could write a narrative or a recount.

This type of title will appeal to you if you have lots of ideas.

This title is about a personal experience, so I should write a recount.

If you find ideas difficult then this might be the title for you. A recount does not have to be a true, real-life event.

I'd have to write a narrative here, with a third-person narrative voice.

If the title tells you which narrative voice to use, you must use it consistently.

Remember that you cannot write a poem or a play in response to this question.

Remember that you should allow 10 minutes for the whole planning process, so this task should take you about 5 minutes.

Now try this

Look closely at the exam-style question on the right. You do not need to write an answer. Instead:

- plan your time as if you were in the exam
- read the question carefully, making notes about the title options
- decide which title you would answer
- note down some ideas (e.g. a spider diagram) about narrative voice and language techniques you could use.

> Choose **one** of the following titles for your writing:
> **Either**, *(a)* My Favourite Room.
> **Or**, *(b)* The Disaster.
> **Or**, *(c)* Write about a visit to a school friend's house.
> **Or**, *(d)* Write a story which begins: I never thought anything could be that amazing… **(40 marks)**

Remember that you cannot write a poem or any other type of verse in response to this question.

Had a look ☐ Nearly there ☐ Nailed it! ☐

Putting it into practice

In **Component 2: Section B – Writing**, you'll need to show you can write for **different purposes and audiences** by answering **two questions**. Before you start writing, think carefully about the questions and plan your time carefully.

Here is one student's exam plan for these questions. Add the missing details.

Timing

Question B1	Question B2
Plan: 5 mins (10.00-10.05)	Plan: 5 mins (10.30-10.35)
Write:	Write: 20 mins (10.30-10.55)
Check:	Check:

Preparing for transactional/persuasive writing

- ✓ Plan your time – you have **1 hour** to answer **both** questions
- ✓ Read the **question** carefully
- ✓ **Annotate** the question to highlight the **form, audience and purpose**
- ✓ **Plan** your writing
- ✓ Prepare to write **300 to 400 words** for **each** answer

Each question deserves the same amount of time as they are both worth 20 marks.

Look carefully at each exam-style question and identify exactly what you are being asked to do. Look at how this student has annotated the key features of these questions:

B1 Your school has announced plans to take part in a student exchange with a school in the USA. The American students will attend your school for six months and an information guide is to be produced to help them settle in.

Write an entry for the information guide explaining what life is like in your school.

You could include:

- details of a typical day
- examples of extra-curricular activities, such as sports and music. **(20 marks)**

Annotations:

- Audience given – teenagers
- Purpose – inform and explain
- Topic – e.g. school life, school day, subjects
- Form – information guide, use headings/sub-headings

B2 A proposal has been made to raise the legal age for driving to 21 years.

You have decided to write to a national newspaper giving your views. You could write in favour of or against this proposal.

Write an interesting and informed article for the newspaper giving your views. (20 marks)

Annotations:

- Topic – driving age, advantages/disadvantages
- Implies audience – mainly adults, need formal style
- Implies purpose – to argue/persuade
- Form – article, needs catchy headline

Now try this

Look closely at these exam-style questions. You do not need to write answers. Instead, draw a four-point spider diagram for **each** one, to identify the audience, purpose, topic and form.

B1 Your local youth club is keen to attract new members.

Write a speech to present to your school's Year 11 assembly persuading students to join the club.

You could write about:

- what the club offers at the moment
- how joining the club would benefit students. **(20 marks)**

B2 A travel website has launched a competition to find the best teenage travel writer.

To enter, teenagers need to write an article for the website about their favourite holiday destination.

Write an engaging article for the website about your favourite holiday destination.

(20 marks)

Form: articles and reviews

In **Component 2: Section B – Writing**, you may be asked to write a newspaper or magazine article, or a review. You need to use the key features of the form you are being asked to write in.

Articles

Headline – gives enough information to engage the reader and may use a pun, alliteration, repetition, rhetorical question, etc.

Sub-heading – gives more information, drawing the reader in.

Quotations from experts make the article seem factual and reliable. Note how speech punctuation is used correctly.

The truth about lying: it's the hands that betray you, not the eyes

By analysing videos of liars, the team found there was no link to their eye movements

ADAM SHERWIN

It is often claimed that even the most stone faced liar will be betrayed by an unwitting eye movement. But new research suggests that 'lying eyes', which no fibber can avoid revealing, are actually a myth. It is actually verbal hesitations and excessive hand gestures that are a better guide.

Prof Wiseman, a psychologist from the University of Hertfordshire, said: 'The results of the first study revealed no relationship between lying and eye movements...'

In the exam you don't need to write the headline in bold block writing. Your normal handwriting will do.

Short opening paragraph – summarises the key points.

Later paragraphs add more detail.

See page 88 for more about punctuation

Reviews

Title of review – usually catchy to engage the reader and indicate the reviewer's opinion.

Rating – gives a view on how good the film or event is.

Engaging opening paragraph – often uses figurative language to give the reader a taste of what the film or event is like.

Transformers: Age of Extinction, review: *'spectacular junk'*

Much like his shape-shifting robot stars, Michael Bay's pulverising Transformers sequel is cinematic treasure disguised as trash, says Robbie Collin.

In Hollywood last week, the skies darkened, the streams ran bitter and a green haze rose from the soil. Strange creatures slunk from the woods, their laughter borne on a foul-smelling wind, and danced horribly while the moon was gibbous.

The new Transformers film, which contains robots that turn into dinosaurs and a weapon that makes people explode, freeze and burst into flames all at the same time, begins with something that is – and there is no other word for it – clever...

Sub-heading – gives more details of the reviewer's opinion.

Further paragraphs add detail and begin to explain the reviewer's opinion.

Note that this structure and organisation is suitable for any type of review. This is for a film, but in the exam you could be asked to review an event or a place.

Now try this

Look at the article and the review on this page. List **three** differences in the features of these two forms.

Had a look ☐ Nearly there ☐ Nailed it! ☐

Form: letters and reports

In **Component 2: Section B – Writing**, you may also be asked to write a letter or a report.

Letters

Your **address** and the **date** go in the top right-hand corner.

The person you are writing to and their address goes on the left, lower down.

Use 'Dear Sir/Madam' if you don't know the name of the person.

Use a **subject** line to draw the reader's immediate attention to your topic – keep the language formal.

Use **Yours faithfully** if you have used 'Dear Sir/Madam'. If you have used the person's name, end with **Yours sincerely**.

57 Woodford Road
Nottingham NG8 4PQ

16 February 2015

The Editor
Nottingham News
17 High Street
Nottingham
NG2 4XY

Dear Sir/Madam

Dog fouling on pavements

It has come to my attention...

and hope that you will take this into account.

Yours faithfully

Jane Smith

Getting it right

In the exam, the most important thing is the quality of your writing. Indicate that it is a letter you are writing – for example, by using 'Dear ...' at the start – but make sure your focus is on the tone and content of your writing.

Reports

Title – formal and factual.

Introduction – two or three sentences giving the main facts about the topic.

Current situation – says what is happening now.

Recommendation – gives an idea about what should change.

Conclusion – summarises what advantages the proposed change will bring.

Reports are information texts and should be formal and factual, but you will probably need to give your opinions as part of the recommendations you make.

See page 52 for more about informative writing

School Marathon Events

Most major cities across the world hold marathon events. These events collect thousands of pounds in sponsorship for charities, from the large, well-known national organisations to small, local ones that are personal to the runners.

Our school currently takes part in national events such as Comic Relief and Children in Need. Such events provide the school with an engaging vehicle for teaching a variety of subjects in a way that engages students of all ages. Last year...

However, whilst they are well supported within the school they do not involve the wider community. A school marathon would create an ideal opportunity to reach out...

So a school marathon event would combine two factors that are essential to a well-rounded education: physical activity and the promotion of empathy.

Now try this

Look at the letter and report on this page. Which form would be most suitable for the following tasks?

1 A letter to your headteacher persuading him/her to relax uniform rules.
2 A proposal to install new fitness equipment in the school gym.
3 An answer to a request from a visiting student for information about your school's library.

Form: information guides

In **Component 2: Section B – Writing**, you may be asked to write an information guide.

Headings and sub-headings

Information guides or leaflets are factual and can carry a lot of information. Use headings and sub-headings to guide the reader through the information.

Use adverbials to link your paragraphs and help guide the reader through your points.

See pages 70 and 71 for more about paragraphing and adverbials

Bullet points and numbered lists

Lists can provide a lot of information in a short space. They can also be used to show ranking or a sequence.

Avoid too many bullet points or numbered lists. You need to show you can structure sentences and paragraphs to guide the reader.

Worked example

B1 Your school is due to take part in an exchange with another school and needs to produce an information guide for the visiting students.

Write an entry for the guide explaining your school's behaviour policy.

You could include:

- examples of school rules
- details of what can go wrong. **(20 marks)**

High School Academy – Behaviour for Beginners

The rules

High School Academy's behaviour policy works because there are only three very simple rules.

1. Always do your best.
2. Always apologise if you are wrong.
3. Always ...

The rules in reality

In reality, there is obviously more to our behaviour policy than just being polite and trying your hardest. Things do go wrong...

Key points to remember

1.
2.
3.

✓ Heading or title – alliteration creates a slightly informal tone suited to the student audience.

✓ Sub-headings structure the text and guide the reader.

✓ A short list – appropriate at the start, but make sure most of your writing shows your skills in using a full variety of sentence structures.

Also see pages 82–84 to revise sentences

✓ Another example of alliteration to engage the audience.

✓ Detailed paragraph with full sentences adds further explanation.

Two or three more sub-headings could be used with a detailed paragraph for each one.

✓ Sub-heading for conclusion – information guides often end with a clear summary of the main points.

Numbered points are used in this conclusion, but you could also use a summary paragraph.

Now try this

Plan your own response to the exam-style question above. Note down:

- a heading
- four or five key sub-headings – don't forget the conclusion!
- where you would use lists or paragraphs.

Don't forget to include a sub-heading for the conclusion.

Putting it into practice

Component 2: Section B – Writing tests your ability to write for **different purposes and audiences**. Look at the exam-style question below and read the extracts from two students' answers.

Worked example

B2 Your local newspaper has published an article criticising local teenagers.

You have decided to write an article in response, arguing that teenagers in fact contribute a lot to society in your local community.

Write an engaging article for the local newspaper giving your views. (20 marks)

Transactional/persuasive writing

For questions like this you should:

- ✓ spend **30 minutes** on your answer, including **planning and checking** time
- ✓ read the **question** carefully and identify the **topic**
- ✓ **annotate** the question to highlight the **form, audience and purpose**
- ✓ **plan** your writing
- ✓ write **300 to 400 words.**

Sample answer

Teenagers – humans or hoodlums?

Not all teenagers hang around on street corners, sipping from bottles of alcohol and spitting on passers-by.

52% of teenagers at our local secondary school have received some form of reward or prize:

- Jane Smith won an art competition.
- Alina Bachar helped her neighbour in the garden.
- Hamid Zaman won first prize in a National Judo competition.

✓ Catchy headline, appropriate for audience.

✗ Opening paragraph does not really say what is positive about teenagers.

✓ Rhetorical device (pattern of three) engages the reader.

✓ Use of statistics appropriate for purpose and form.

✗ The list is not suitable; articles need to have fully developed paragraphs.

Improved sample answer

Teenagers – dangerous or diligent?

A regular reader of this newspaper may well feel that all teenagers hang around on street corners, sipping from bottles of alcohol and spitting on passers-by. This image sells newspapers. But is it the whole story?

Positive stories do exist. I know of more teenagers who get it right than get it wrong. Some readers may choose to buy into the idea that all teenagers are trouble. However, take John Jones, for instance. Rather than idling on street corners, John has spent the last year giving up every weekend to help...

✓ Rhetorical question engages the reader.

✓ Opening paragraph summarises the key points.

✓ Developed paragraph details first key point of argument.

✓ The adverbial 'however' dismisses this well-placed counter-argument.

Now try this

In your own response to the exam-style question above, write:

- a headline
- a sub-heading
- a short opening paragraph
- one developed paragraph about your first key point.

Try to include techniques that match the purpose, for example, rhetorical devices, evidence, counter-argument and adverbials.

Ideas and planning: creative

For **Component 1: Section B – Writing** you will need to produce a piece of **creative prose writing**. Planning is the only way to produce a well-structured and fully developed piece of writing.

Title options

You will be given **four title options** for the writing task in **Component 1**. For example:

Choose **one** of the following titles for your writing: **(40 marks)**

Either, *(a)* The Storm.

Or, *(b)* The Choice.

Or, *(c)* Write about a time when you were scared.

Or, *(d)* Write a story which begins: The door swung shut, leaving me alone...

Choose a title as quickly as you can to maximise time for planning! Which do you have the most initial ideas about?

Getting it right

For the **creative prose writing** task in **Component 1** you should spend around 10 minutes planning before you start to write.

See page 49 to refresh your memory about Component 1: Section B – Writing

Ideas – picturing it

Ask yourself:

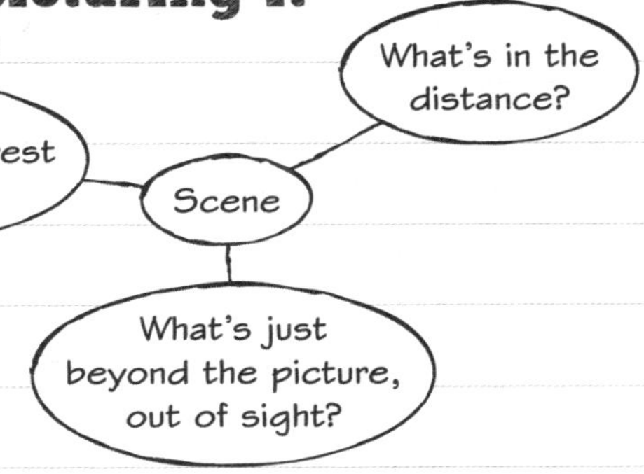

- Scene
  - What's nearest to me?
  - What's in the distance?
  - What's just beyond the picture, out of sight?

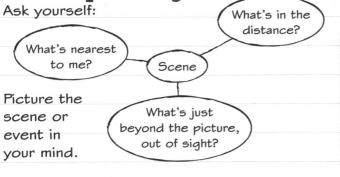

Picture the scene or event in your mind.

Ideas – what's happening?

Think about the characters and action:

Characters
Who's there? Who are they? What are they like? How do they feel? Why?

Action
What is happening? What are the characters doing? What happened before? What will happen next?

Planning

Titles like 'The Choice' need a lot of **imagination**. Remember to **stay focused** on the title. A **spider diagram** keeps your ideas centred on the **main idea**:

- The Choice: summer holiday or volunteering
  - Dream of holiday – use five senses to describe destination
  - Mum offers choice, describe mood when choosing volunteering, proud but despondent at same time, use dialogue to show Mum's character
  - Homeless shelter – describe atmosphere, use personification?
  - Mysterious stranger at volunteering, shock that he is young & attractive, use similes/metaphors to describe eyes & clothing

When you have your basic ideas, think about how to develop them into four or five paragraphs. Remember to include creative writing techniques. Can you spot any in this plan?

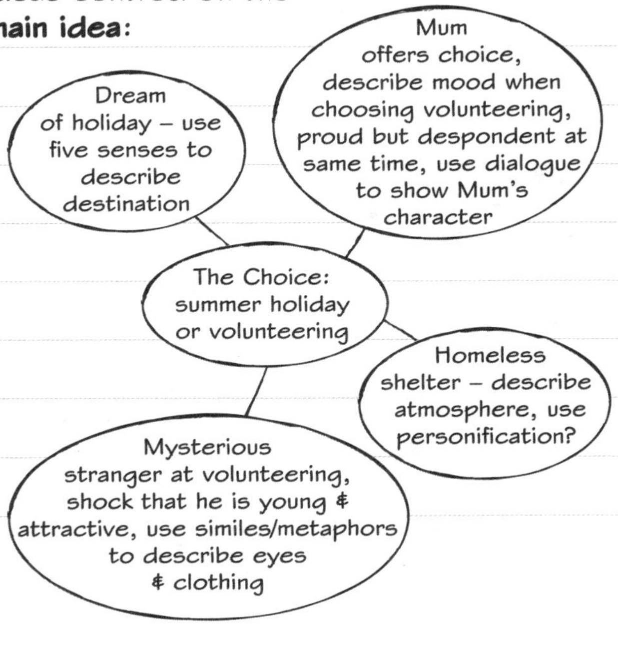

Now try this

Choose one of the following exam-style title options for your writing. Plan your ideas for **four** or **five** paragraphs using **one** of the methods above.

The Storm. Making a Difference. Finding a Friend.

Remember that you have 10 minutes in total to plan your answer for this type of question, so spend about 5 minutes gathering ideas for this task.

Structure: creative

For **Component 1: Section B – Writing** you will need to structure your **creative prose writing** effectively. It is often best to use some type of **narrative structure**.

Narrative structure

In the exam, you are most likely to write a short story. Short stories work best when they use a simple five-part structure like this:

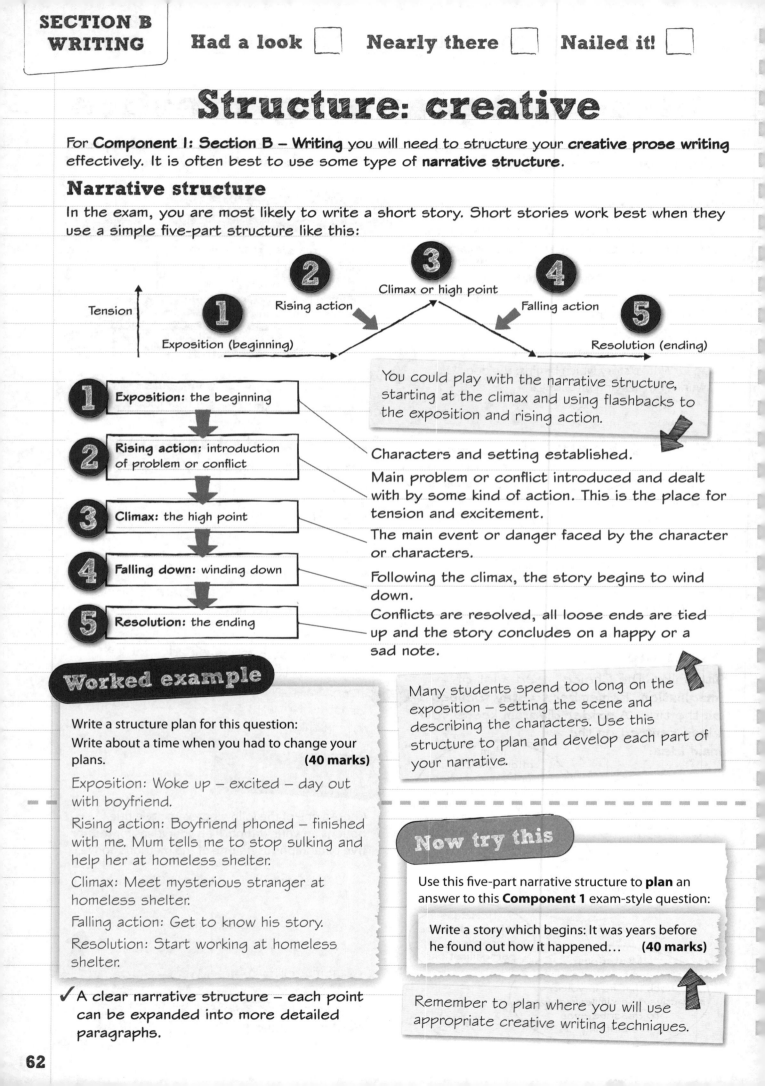

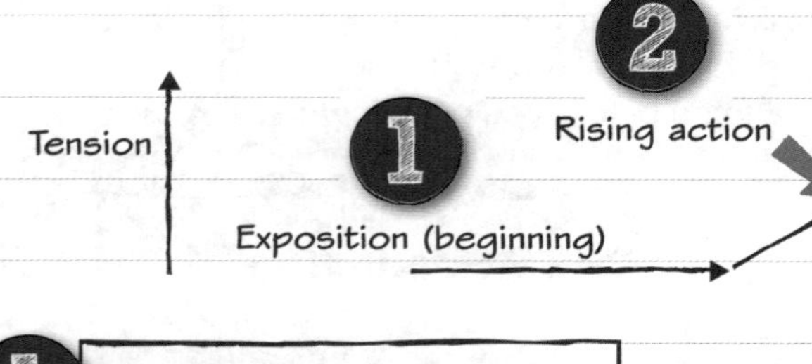

1. **Exposition:** the beginning – Characters and setting established.
2. **Rising action:** introduction of problem or conflict – Main problem or conflict introduced and dealt with by some kind of action. This is the place for tension and excitement.
3. **Climax:** the high point – The main event or danger faced by the character or characters.
4. **Falling down:** winding down – Following the climax, the story begins to wind down.
5. **Resolution:** the ending – Conflicts are resolved, all loose ends are tied up and the story concludes on a happy or a sad note.

You could play with the narrative structure, starting at the climax and using flashbacks to the exposition and rising action.

Many students spend too long on the exposition – setting the scene and describing the characters. Use this structure to plan and develop each part of your narrative.

Worked example

Write a structure plan for this question:
Write about a time when you had to change your plans. **(40 marks)**

Exposition: Woke up – excited – day out with boyfriend.

Rising action: Boyfriend phoned – finished with me. Mum tells me to stop sulking and help her at homeless shelter.

Climax: Meet mysterious stranger at homeless shelter.

Falling action: Get to know his story.

Resolution: Start working at homeless shelter.

✓ A clear narrative structure – each point can be expanded into more detailed paragraphs.

Now try this

Use this five-part narrative structure to **plan** an answer to this **Component 1** exam-style question:

Write a story which begins: It was years before he found out how it happened… **(40 marks)**

Remember to plan where you will use appropriate creative writing techniques.

Beginnings and endings: creative

The **beginning** and **ending** of a piece of **creative prose writing** are very important. Both need to have an **impact** on the reader.

The beginning

The beginning needs to:

- engage the reader immediately
- set the tone for the rest of the writing.

There are several ways you can do this: with a vivid description, with dialogue, with a mystery, with conflict or danger.

The beginning is sometimes called the 'exposition' or 'opening'.

With a vivid description

Glistening and gleaming in the evening haze, the sea spread out before us like a silver carpet. Waves lapped gently at the sides of the boat as we she sailed silently along in the cool, salty breeze.

A good way to start if the setting plays a big role in your narrative or recount.

Opportunities to show your skills with creative writing techniques like figurative language.

With dialogue

'I'm scared. What do we do now?' Shadows flickered on Sarah's terrified face as she whispered her fears. 'Nothing.' He hissed. 'Keep quiet and just wait.'

Gives the reader an immediate idea about one or more important characters.

With a mystery

I know I shouldn't have taken it. But I did. I'll be sorry for the rest of my miserable little life. It was only a little thing – but it caused so much trouble.

An engaging way to start if you want to use flashbacks.

The ending

The ending is the final impression the reader has of your writing. Follow the rules below for a strong ending.

- **Plan** each stage of your writing in advance – you will be less likely to run out of time and rush at the end.
- Spend time thinking about the **tone** of your ending – will it be happy, sad or funny?
- Craft your **final sentence** carefully – this is the last bit of your writing an examiner will read.
- Avoid sudden mood changes – if the mood has been tense throughout, a happy ending is unlikely to work.
- Avoid ending with a cliché like 'it was all a dream' – use your imagination!

With conflict or danger

I froze. Someone was in the house. I couldn't see them. But I knew they were there.

An effective way to create a sense of tension from the start.

Now try this

Here is a title for a **Component 1** exam-style task:

Home Alone. **(40 marks)**

1 Write **four** possible openings using the techniques above. Use a different technique for each opening.

2 Choose **one** of your openings and write the **final paragraph**.

Had a look ☐ Nearly there ☐ Nailed it! ☐

Putting it into practice

Component 1: Section B – Writing tests your **creative prose writing** skills. Planning before you write will help you produce a stronger answer. Look at the exam-style question below and the two students' plans.

Planning for creative writing

To plan for a question like this you should:

- ✓ spend 10 minutes planning your answer – the more detailed your plan is, the stronger your answer will be
- ✓ read each title option carefully
- ✓ decide which title to answer
- ✓ plan narrative voice and creative writing techniques you will use
- ✓ create a full and detailed plan.

Worked example

Write a story which begins: Opening the door changed his life forever... **(40 marks)**

Sample plan

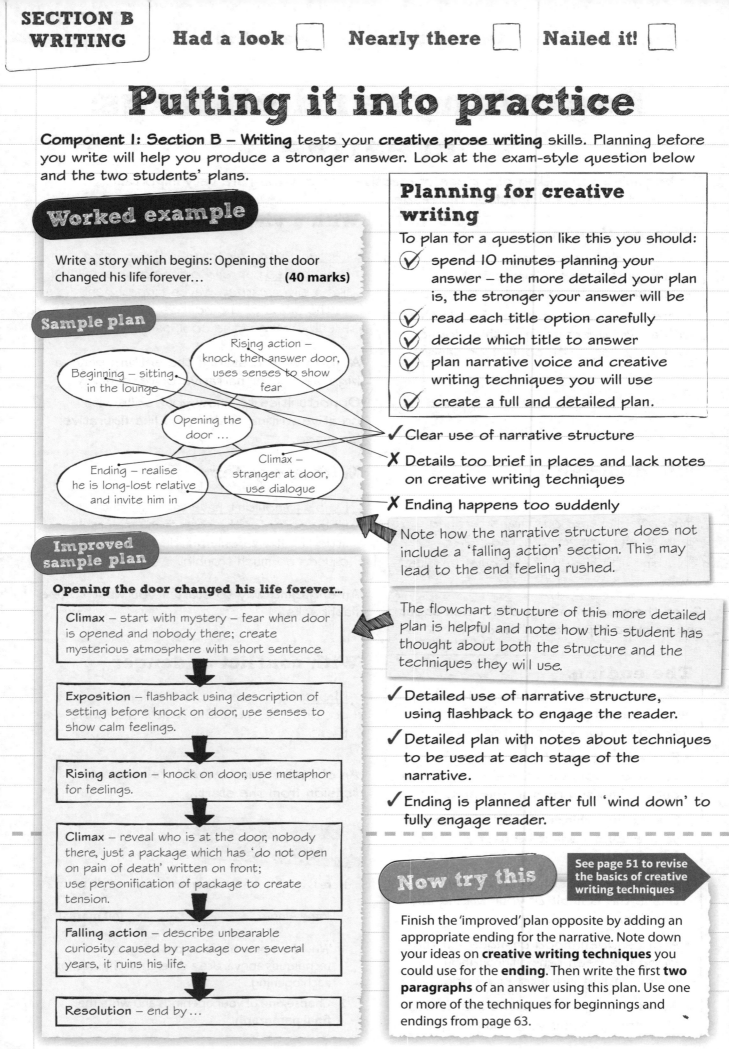

Opening the door ...

- Beginning – sitting in the lounge
- Rising action – knock, then answer door, uses senses to show fear
- Climax – stranger at door, use dialogue
- Ending – realise he is long-lost relative and invite him in

✓ Clear use of narrative structure

✗ Details too brief in places and lack notes on creative writing techniques

✗ Ending happens too suddenly

Note how the narrative structure does not include a 'falling action' section. This may lead to the end feeling rushed.

Improved sample plan

Opening the door changed his life forever...

Climax – start with mystery – fear when door is opened and nobody there; create mysterious atmosphere with short sentence.

↓

Exposition – flashback using description of setting before knock on door, use senses to show calm feelings.

↓

Rising action – knock on door, use metaphor for feelings.

↓

Climax – reveal who is at the door, nobody there, just a package which has 'do not open on pain of death' written on front; use personification of package to create tension.

↓

Falling action – describe unbearable curiosity caused by package over several years, it ruins his life.

↓

Resolution – end by ...

The flowchart structure of this more detailed plan is helpful and note how this student has thought about both the structure and the techniques they will use.

✓ Detailed use of narrative structure, using flashback to engage the reader.

✓ Detailed plan with notes about techniques to be used at each stage of the narrative.

✓ Ending is planned after full 'wind down' to fully engage reader.

Now try this

See page 51 to revise the basics of creative writing techniques

Finish the 'improved' plan opposite by adding an appropriate ending for the narrative. Note down your ideas on **creative writing techniques** you could use for the **ending**. Then write the first **two paragraphs** of an answer using this plan. Use one or more of the techniques for beginnings and endings from page 63.

Ideas and planning: inform, explain, review

Component 2: Section B – Writing tests your skills in writing for **different audiences and purposes**. Planning your answer will help you to choose the **form**, **features** and **techniques** that best suit the task's **audience and purpose**.

Plan an introduction that says what you are writing about and why it is important.

You will need three or four **key points**. These should be your main ideas.

Add ideas to each of your **key points**.

Use temporal (time) adverbials to guide your reader through your points.

Use **appropriate techniques** to support the **audience and purpose**.

Worked example

B1 Your local council is keen to improve facilities for young people.

Write an informative report for the council explaining how the facilities could be improved.

You could include:

- what is available at the moment
- your ideas about how current facilities could be improved
- your ideas about new facilities. **(20 marks)**

Plan

Intro

- Firstly... not enough facilities
- need to improve them
- stop teenagers causing problems in town – ~~could include~~ statistics of recent trouble

1 Key point – **Existing facilities**

- facts – what is available now
- poor condition – give example of astro-turf & use expert opinion

2 Key point – **Improvements suggested**

- youth club – redecorate, could ask teenagers to help?
- repair astro-turf, get grant from sports company
- add computers to local library

3 Key point – **New facilities**

- bowling alley, give an estimate of how much money this could bring in
- coffee shop – could be run by volunteers

Conclusion

- Finally... explain benefit to other local people

You might want to change the order of your paragraphs once you have written your plan.

Getting it right

Remember that you will need to answer **both** questions for **Component 2: Section B – Writing**.

- You have **one hour** to complete **both** tasks.
- You should spend **5 minutes planning** for **each** question – you could choose to plan both answers at the beginning, and then spend 25 minutes on each answer.
- One question will have bullet points – use them to help you with ideas!

Now try this

Look at this exam-style question and plan an answer:

B1 Your school is considering the creation of a youth club facility to be open at lunchtimes, and after school.

Write a report for the Headteacher explaining why a youth club facility would be a good idea.

You could write about:

- what activities could be provided by the youth club
- why a youth club would benefit the whole school. **(20 marks)**

Think carefully about the structure and the features and techniques you need to include to suit the audience and purpose.

Had a look ☐ Nearly there ☐ Nailed it! ☐

Ideas and planning: argue and persuade

Planning is the only way to produce a well-structured piece of writing, full of relevant imaginative ideas and carefully crafted language. It will help you to **structure** your **transactional writing** for **Component 2: Section B – Writing** in a logical way that helps the reader to follow your ideas.

Worked example

B2 The national press has been debating whether or not watching television is a waste of time. You have decided to write an article for a national newspaper giving your views. You could write in agreement with the idea that television is a waste of time, or against it.

Write a thoughtful article for the newspaper giving your views. **(20 marks)**

Plan: TV is stealing your life

Intro
100s of channels run all day and all night
Average person watches 4 hours a day – a quarter of their waking life!

2 TV is passive not active
Evidence: my sister – hours spent staring, doing nothing.
Overweight and silent, TV is killing her brain and body.

3 TV is addictive
Once you start, it's difficult to turn off.
Evidence: watch whatever is on, not choosing what to watch.

~~Advertising is annoying~~
~~10/15 mins of it every hour – they want my money!~~

4 Families don't talk anymore
Evidence: Mine eats dinner in silence in front of the telly.

5 Some say it's educational and entertaining
It can be both – but how often? More often it's neither – e.g. Big Brother.

Conclusion
Most telly is a waste of time for everyone.
Choose what you want to watch – then turn it off.

If the question gives you a choice, decide whether you are **for** or **against**. Remember to give your writing a title that reflects your point of view.

Don't be afraid to cross out some of your ideas.

Write your introduction, telling the reader what the situation is at the moment, and why that is a problem they need to think about.

Add some evidence to support each key point you make. **Plan key points** by gathering together all the different ideas you can think of that support your viewpoint.

Choose and sequence the most persuasive points. You will probably only need two or three key points.

Don't stop when you've thought of three ideas. Think of more, reject weaker ideas, then put the strong ideas in a logical order.

Add a counter-argument that gives an opposing viewpoint. Then say why you disagree.

Plan a conclusion – your final point to hammer home your argument.

Now try this

Write a plan for the **other** side of the argument, arguing that television is **not** a waste of time.

Openings: transactional/ persuasive

Starting a piece of writing can be difficult. For **Component 2: Section B – Writing**, know what you want to write, or you will be in danger of writing one or two boring paragraphs before you really get going.

An effective opening

Your first paragraph of any writing task – and your first sentence in particular – needs to grab the reader's interest and attention. You could use one or more of these five ideas.

- A bold and / or controversial statement:

> Experimenting on animals is a cruel necessity.

- A relevant quotation:

> 'What's in a name? That which we call a rose by any other name would smell as sweet.'
> (William Shakespeare, *Romeo and Juliet*, 2.2)

- A shocking or surprising fact or statistic:

> 99 per cent of the species that have ever lived on Planet Earth are now extinct.

- A rhetorical question:

> How many of us can honestly say that we care more about others than we do about ourselves?

- A short, relevant, **interesting** anecdote:

> When I was seven, my parents bought me a dog. This was when I first realised that …

Introducing your topic

After your opening sentence, go on to introduce what you are writing about.

> … The average person spends a quarter of their waking life watching television. Are they making good use of their time? Or is television sucking the life out of them, killing them slowly with its mind-numbing mediocrity?

A surprising statistic shocks the reader and grabs their attention. Here, it invites the reader to compare how long they spend watching TV.

Two questions engage the reader, and present the two sides of the argument. The second question makes it clear which side the writer is on.

Getting it right

Avoid telling the reader what you are going to write about:
In this essay I am going to argue that television is not a waste of time.
Just write it:
Television is informative, educational and interesting.

Now try this

Look at the exam-style question opposite:

1 Write **three** possible openings that would grab your reader's attention from the start.

2 Choose the most effective opening, then complete the introduction.

B2 A proposal has been made to build a skateboard ramp in your local park.
You have decided to write an article for your local community website giving your views. You could write in favour or against the proposal.
Write an engaging article for the website giving your views. (20 marks)

Had a look ☐ Nearly there ☐ Nailed it! ☐

Conclusions: transactional/ persuasive

For **Component 2: Section B – Writing**, plan your conclusion before you start writing. Your final paragraph should leave your reader with a lasting impression.

Summing up

Plan your conclusion before you start writing. The final paragraph or conclusion to a text can be used to sum up your ideas – but avoid repeating them. Instead, aim to sum up and emphasise your central idea. You could use one or more of these things.

End on a vivid image: a picture that lingers in the reader's mind. A homeless person sits cold and alone in a shop doorway. As you pass by, you look into her eyes. She can't be older than 15.	**End on a warning:** what will happen if your ideas are not acted on? Within 50 years, the world will have changed beyond all recognition – and our children will blame us for what has happened.	**End on a happy note:** emphasise how great things will be if your ideas are acted on. Ours could be the generation that made the difference.
End on a thought-provoking question: leave the reader thinking. For how long can we ignore what is staring us in the face?	**Refer back to your introduction**, but don't repeat it. I still have that dog – and he's still incredibly badly behaved. But if I hadn't …	**End on a call to action:** make it clear what you want the reader to do. Don't just sit there. Get up, get out and make it happen.

Worked example

Remember that questions engage the reader with the issue – how does it relate to their own life?

B2 The national press has been debating whether or not watching television is a waste of time. You have decided to write an article for a national newspaper giving your views. You could write in agreement with the idea that television is a waste of time, or against it.

Write a thoughtful article for the newspaper giving your views. **(20 marks)**

How many hours of television have you watched this week? What else could you have done with those hours? Television has turned us all into spectators - and while we're glued to the box, our lives are ticking away, wasted and unused. It's time to stop watching. It's time to start taking part.

A warning.

A final, powerful call to action.

This is an example of a conclusion.

Now try this

Look at the exam-style question opposite. Choose **one or more** of the above techniques to write a powerful conclusion.

B2 A proposal has been made to build a skateboard ramp in your local park. You have decided to write an article for your local community website giving your views. You could write in favour or against the proposal.

Write an engaging article for the website giving your views. **(20 marks)**

Putting it into practice

Component 2: Section B – Writing tests your skills in writing for **different audiences and purposes.** Planning before you write will help you produce stronger answers. Look at the exam-style question below and the two students' plans.

Worked example

B1 Your local newspaper has started a travel section and has invited readers to contribute.

Write a review for the local newspaper of a place you have visited.

You could write about:

- a town or an attraction such as a museum or theme park
- what makes the place particularly enjoyable to visit. **(20 marks)**

You need to write 300 to 400 words to answer this question.

Planning for transactional/ persuasive writing

To plan for a question like this you should:

- ✓ spend about **5 minutes planning** each answer
- ✓ read the **question** carefully and identify the **topic**
- ✓ **annotate** the question to highlight the **form, audience and purpose**
- ✓ **plan** the features and techniques you will use to support the **form, audience and purpose**
- ✓ create a **full and detailed plan.**

Sample plan

Bradcaster Park

- Good, fun, interesting.
- Playground for kids.
- Lake
-

✓ Some language ideas but undeveloped / unambitious

✓ Some ideas gathered, but more needed

Make sure you provide a range of details for questions like this. In this plan there is no detail added about the lake, the information about the park is not sequenced, and there is no introduction or conclusion.

Improved sample plan

Goose Fair: 700 years of family fun!

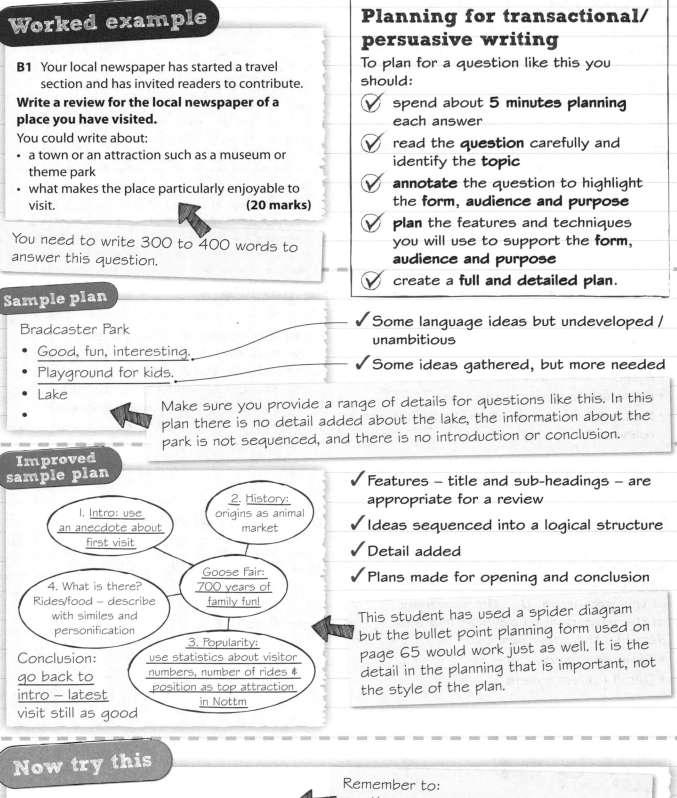

1. Intro: use an anecdote about first visit

2. History: origins as animal market

3. Popularity: use statistics about visitor numbers, number of rides & position as top attraction in Nottm

4. What is there? Rides/food – describe with similes and personification

Conclusion: go back to intro – latest visit still as good

✓ Features – title and sub-headings – are appropriate for a review

✓ Ideas sequenced into a logical structure

✓ Detail added

✓ Plans made for opening and conclusion

This student has used a spider diagram but the bullet point planning form used on page 65 would work just as well. It is the detail in the planning that is important, not the style of the plan.

Now try this

Plan your answer to the above exam-style question and write an opening paragraph.

Remember to:

- gather, organise and sequence your ideas
- plan your introduction and conclusion.

Had a look ☐ Nearly there ☐ Nailed it! ☐

Paragraphing for effect

The best answers are organised into **paragraphs**. They help **structure** your writing, making it easier for the reader to follow your thinking and absorb your ideas. You will need to use paragraphs for your writing in **both components**.

Paragraphing for effect

In most cases you should start a new paragraph each time you start a new point. However, you can use shorter paragraphs for effect: to emphasise a point or create a dramatic pause.

A one-sentence paragraph can create a sense of tension and pace. Here, it leaves the reader in suspense about what actually happens to Ben. This will make them want to continue reading.

> Settling in front of the fire, Ben kicked off his shoes and stretched out his toes towards the warmth. Outside, rain battered the windows, through which he could just make out the autumn leaves as they danced around the garden and settled on the surface of the pond. Today was a good day to stay inside and relax.
>
> Later, Ben was to see that moment as his last real taste of freedom.
>
> The day had started much like any other. He had eaten his cereal, brushed his teeth, checked his bag and then left for school.

Structuring paragraphs: argue and persuade

Use Point-Evidence-Explanation to structure paragraphs in a piece of writing to argue or persuade.

- A short, clear **point**.
- **Evidence** to support the point.
- **Explains** how the point and evidence are relevant to the main idea.

> Britain's weather is changing. Barely a month goes by without it being declared the wettest, the driest, the hottest, the coldest, or the windiest month on record. Our weather is clearly becoming more extreme, and is likely to become even more so. How long can we ignore this before we act?

Structuring paragraphs: inform, explain, review

Start each paragraph with a **topic sentence** – a sentence that clearly introduces the reader to the content of this paragraph. Use the remainder of the paragraph to develop and add detail to the topic sentence.

- Topic sentence
- Detail / development

> Our school has made a huge effort to recycle its waste. Every classroom has a bin just for waste paper, which is collected each week by student volunteers. In the canteen, we sort our rubbish into plastics, tin cans, and food waste. Even the staff room has three different bins so teachers can recycle!

Now try this

Write the next paragraph to either of the student answers above.

Linking ideas

Adverbials can be used to **guide** the reader through your ideas. They can work like **signposts**, showing the reader the direction your ideas are taking. Use adverbials to improve your writing for **both components**.

Adding an idea

- Moreover …
- Furthermore …
- In addition …

This will not solve the situation. **Moreover**, it could make it worse.

Furthermore, this is likely to interrupt students' learning and add to their stress levels.

Explaining

- As a result
- Therefore
- Consequently

Science suggests that the teenage brain needs more sleep to help it grow and develop. **Consequently**, we spend longer in bed.

Teenagers' attitudes and actions are constantly challenged. It is **therefore** unsurprising that they sometimes challenge those who challenge them.

Illustrating

- For example
- For instance

For example, teenagers are frequently assumed to be responsible for graffiti and vandalism.

Emphasising

- In particular
- Especially
- Significantly

Significantly, these problems increased when the youth club was shut down.

Time or **temporal** adverbials are very useful for indicating the passage of time in creative writing.

Comparing and contrasting

Comparing	**Contrasting**
Similarly	However
Likewise	On the other hand
In the same way	On the contrary

It has been argued that an animal's life is not as valuable as that of a human being. **Similarly**, some have said that animals exist only because humans need them as a source of food. **However**, I would like to stress that…

Showing time

- Afterwards
- At this moment
- Before
- Previously
- After a while
- Then
- Later
- Meanwhile

Immediately **afterwards** he was to wonder what all the fuss had been about. **After a while** he was even able to see that he had dramatically over-reacted. But at the point when the door swung open, Ben had no thought in his head beyond…

Now try this

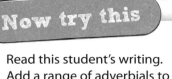

Read this student's writing. Add a range of adverbials to link the ideas together and guide the reader through them.

This morning, my sister proved that she is the most annoying person on earth. She finished all the milk so there was none left for me. She spent an hour in the bathroom. She borrowed my headphones without asking and wouldn't give them back. She can be thoughtful. She made me a delicious lasagne the other day. She always remembers my birthday and buys me great presents.

Had a look ☐ Nearly there ☐ Nailed it! ☐

Putting it into practice

Worked example

B1 Your local newspaper is running a campaign to encourage older people to use modern technology.

Write an article for the newspaper persuading older people of the benefits of modern technology.

You could write about:

- what types of technology they could use
- how the technology will make their lives easier
- where to get help with modern technology.

(20 marks)

For **both components**, you need to structure your writing in a way that makes it easy for the reader to follow. Using paragraphs and adverbials will help you to do this. Look at the **Component 2** exam-style question and read the extracts from two students' answers.

Paragraphing and adverbials

For each writing question you should:

- ✓ write in paragraphs
- ✓ plan one point per paragraph
- ✓ use adverbials to guide your reader through the text.

Sample answer extract

One of the most popular things you can do on the internet is social networking. You can go on websites like Facebook and keep in touch with all your friends. You can also use online encyclopedias to find out about anything you want to know. You can also use the internet to save your photos and share them with your friends and relatives on websites like Facebook, which links back to what I was saying before.

✓ A clear point supported with evidence

✗ This evidence should be supported with a persuasive explanation.

✗ This point should have been sequenced to develop the first point, using an adverbial to guide the reader.

Remember that a new point should mean a new paragraph. Remember also to support your points with evidence or an explanation. This point contains neither.

Improved sample answer

The internet is a modern miracle: a world of information at your fingertips, waiting to be discovered. Thanks to clever websites called 'search engines', all you have to do is type in a few words and up will pop an enormous choice of websites, all ready to tell you what you want to know. It's so simple, you'll be surfing the internet before you know it.

There are hundreds of things you can do on a computer as well as accessing the internet. For example, you can email friends and relations around the world, sharing your news and views in just a few clicks. It's much quicker than writing a letter – and you don't have to pay a fortune for a stamp, so it can even save you money.

✓ Paragraph clearly organised using:

- point
- evidence
- explanation.

Note the accurate paragraphing with links back to the previous paragraph and also the adverbial (For example) to introduce evidence.

Now try this

Remember to:

- write in paragraphs
- use P-E-E to structure your paragraphs
- use adverbials.

Plan and write the next two paragraphs of the 'Improved sample answer' above. Use the bullet points in the question to help you with ideas.

Vocabulary for effect: synonyms

Synonyms are words with similar meanings. Use them in your writing for **both components** to avoid repetition and to add variety.

Using synonyms can make your writing more varied and interesting. Having a range of synonyms for key words and ideas in mind as you write will mean that:

- you don't repeat the same key word throughout your writing
- you can pick the most precise word – the one that really says what you want it to say.

Be your own thesaurus

You know hundreds – perhaps thousands – of words that you rarely use. So you don't need a thesaurus to come up with ambitious, effective vocabulary chosen for its impact. You just need to think through your mental thesaurus. Beware though! Don't use a word if you are not absolutely sure of its precise meaning.

Examples of synonyms

Comments on evidence often involve the phrase This suggests … Replace it with:

- This gives the impression that …
- It seems clear that …
- This implies …
- In other words …

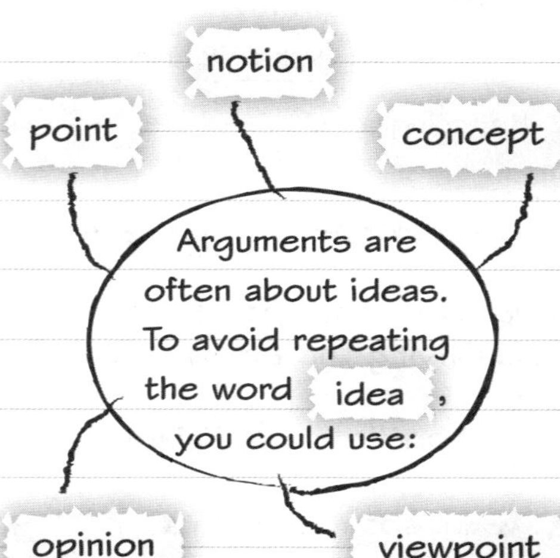

Worked example

B2 A national newspaper has asked for views from the public on whether or not celebrities make good models for young people.

You have decided to write to the newspaper giving your views. You could argue in favour of the idea that celebrities are good role models, or against it.

Write a letter to the newspaper giving your views. **(20 marks)**

The idea of celebrities as perfect role models is not the only misguided idea connected with the world of the celebrity. Some people have the idea that celebrities should be consulted on everything from international politics to haircare.

Repetition can add pace and rhythm to your writing – but there are too many words being repeated too often here, weakening an otherwise strong paragraph.

Getting it right

Using the same word more than once can undo all the hard word you put into an answer, making your ideas seem repetitive and uninteresting.

Now try this

Before you start, make a list of all the synonyms you can think of for the word 'celebrity'. You can use a thesaurus if you get stuck.

Rewrite the 'Worked example answer' opposite, replacing the words 'celebrities', 'celebrity' and 'idea' with different synonyms.

Had a look ☐ Nearly there ☐ Nailed it! ☐

Vocabulary for effect: argue and persuade

When writing to **argue or persuade** in **Component 2: Section B – Writing**, you need to be able to use a wide vocabulary of **emotive words** and **positive and negative language**.

Vocabulary for impact

Using emotive language can add impact to your argument. For example, you may think that global warming is a problem. To shock your reader into action, you want to emphasise the problem by choosing a more emotive word:

If we ignore global warming now, we will soon be facing a ~~problem.~~

catastrophe. | disaster. | calamity.

Add even more power to your sentence by intensifying the emotive word:

horrific | alarming | terrifying

we will soon be facing a terrifying catastrophe.

Positive and negative

If you frame your ideas in **positive** or **negative** language you can control your reader's reaction to them. For example:

If you **support** fox hunting, it could be described as: 'A humane method of pest control'.

If you **oppose** fox hunting, it could be described as: 'A cruel and barbaric sport'.

If you are arguing in **support** of typical teenage behaviour, you could point out that: 'Sleep is an essential ingredient for the teenage brain's development.'

Taking the **opposing point of view** you might write: 'Idle teenagers lounge in bed for hours, paralysed by their crippling laziness.'

Connotations

You can guide your reader's reaction by thinking about the connotations of your vocabulary choice. Look at these words. Each one has a similar meaning but carries different associations.

Six hours of intensive revision can make you

- exhausted. — extreme, intense
- drained. — implies weak, empty
- sleepy. — sounds childish, mocking

Fox hunting is

- brutal. — emphasises violence
- barbaric. — suggests uncivilised
- heartless. — emphasises lack of feeling or empathy

Now try this

Write an opening paragraph for the exam-style question opposite, focusing on vocabulary to persuade the reader.

Remember to choose vocabulary for its impact and for its connotations.

B2 The editor of your school newspaper has asked for contributions in response to this topic: 'School is cruel'.

You have decided to write an article to share your views on this topic. You could write in favour of the statement, or against it.

Write a lively article for the school newspaper giving your views. (20 marks)

Language for different effects 1

Language techniques can add **power** and **impact** to your writing. These techniques will mainly be useful for your transactional writing for **Component 2**, but you could also use them in your creative prose writing for **Component 1**.

Rhetorical questions

Use these in argument or persuasive writing to lead the reader to the answer you want.

There is really only one way to answer these questions:

Who in their right mind would do such a thing?

Would you stand by and do nothing if you saw a human being treated like this?

You can also use them in creative writing to engage the reader in a situation:

What was going on?

What should I do?

Contrast

Place two opposing ideas or situations in direct contrast to emphasise the difference.

You can work hard in a job you hate for the rest of your life

or you can work hard on your GCSEs for a couple of years and get the job you want.

You can also use contrast in creative writing to exaggerate a detail: 'Among all the smiling, happy faces there was just one exception: my father's sour-faced, snarling scowl.'

Repetition

Repeating a word or phrase can emphasise a key point or idea in an argument:

Chasing a helpless animal across open country is cruel. Setting a pack of dogs on a helpless animal is cruel. Watching as the dogs butcher the helpless animal is cruel.

It can also add emphasis to an idea in creative writing:

There is no point in discussing it, there is no point in arguing about it, there is no point in shouting about it. Once my father has made up his mind, it is made up.

Lists

Use a list to suggest a range of ideas in your persuasive writing:

It's quick, simple, easy and cheap.

The improvement would be huge: students would learn more, learn faster, be more motivated, enjoy school more and achieve better results.

Use it to suggest range or variety in your descriptive writing.

Scattered across the carpet were balloons, paper hats, lumps of cake, streamers and torn shreds of wrapping paper.

Now try this

Choose **one** of these exam-style questions.

Component 1:

Write about a time when you visited your favourite place. **(40 marks)**

Component 2:

B1 Your school is keen to encourage students to take more physical exercise.

Write a report for the Headteacher suggesting ways this might be done.

You could include:

- examples of activities available now
- examples of additional activities that could be provided. **(20 marks)**

Write **four** short extracts from your chosen task. Use **one** of the language techniques above in each task.

Had a look ☐ Nearly there ☐ Nailed it! ☐

Language for different effects 2

Language techniques can add **power** and **impact** to your writing. These techniques will mainly be useful for your transactional writing for **Component 2**, but you could also use them in your creative prose writing for **Component 1**.

Direct address

For **Component 2: Section B – Writing** questions, talking directly to the reader can be very persuasive.

'**you** can get involved in lots of different ways'

this involves the reader and is much more persuasive than:

'There are many ways to get involved.'

Using the **first person plural 'we'** can create a relationship between you, the writer, and the reader. It suggests that we are all in the same situation, facing the same problems:

'If **we** do nothing, then nothing will change. It is up to us to act and act now.'

Pattern of three

Putting words or phrases in linked groups of three adds rhythm and emphasis to your ideas in all kinds of writing:

It doesn't matter if you're a beginner, an improver, or an expert. It's fun for everyone!

It will benefit the students, the teachers, and the community as a whole.

I approached the front door. My hands were cold, clammy and shaking.

Alliteration

Alliteration can add rhythm and emphasis to your writing. Remember: the alliterative words do not have to be *next* to each other – just *near* each other.

It was a truly terrifying experience.

Combined with other language techniques, alliteration can be particularly engaging and powerful: 'It's fun, fast and furious.'

Hyperbole

Exaggeration can:

- add humour to an argument or a description:

The house looked like a herd of elephants had run through it, detonating hand grenades as they went.

- emphasise a key point:

Teachers want their students to sit completely still and in total silence for six hours a day.

Now try this

Choose **one** of these exam-style questions.

Component 1:

Write about a time when you felt under pressure. **(40 marks)**

Component 2:

B2 Your local newspaper has published an article suggesting that mobile phones are killing young people's ability to communicate. You have decided to write to the newspaper giving your views on this subject. You could write in favour or against the view given in the newspaper.

Write a lively article for the newspaper giving your views. (20 marks)

Write **four** short extracts from your chosen task, using **one** of the language techniques above in each.

Language for different effects 3

You can use **figurative language** to create powerful images in your readers' minds. You should certainly use figurative language in your **creative prose writing** for **Component 1**. If you use it carefully (and not too often!), figurative language can also show your originality in the **transactional writing tasks** in **Component 2**.

Similes

A simile is a comparison, usually using **as** or **like**, suggesting a resemblance between one thing and another. It can be used:

- **to inform**

> When you get it right, skateboarding can be as exhilarating as a skydive from 30,000 feet.

- **to persuade**

> Smoking cigarettes is like a game of Russian roulette – and the chances are, you'll end up losing.

Metaphors

A metaphor is a direct comparison suggesting a resemblance between one thing and another. It can be used:

- **to argue**

> At night, when there is nothing else to do, the youth club is a bright light in the darkness, drawing all the young people of the town through its doors.

- **to describe**

> She stared and stared, her eyes burning holes in my face.

Personification

Personification is the technique of describing something non-human as if it were human. It can be used when writing:

- **to describe**

> Sunlight danced on the water as we headed out to sea.

- **to persuade**

> Smoking is highly addictive and, once the habit has got its hands around your throat, it will not let go.

Getting it right

- **Don't** try to force one simile, one metaphor **and** one personification into each answer.
- **Do** use figurative language in your transactional writing for **Component 2**, but **don't** overdo it.
- **Do** look for opportunities where figurative language will add impact to your ideas.
- **Do** avoid clichés – try to be original.

Avoiding clichés

While an imaginative and original simile or metaphor can add greatly to your writing, a cliché can destroy the effect. So **do not** describe someone as:

- cool as a cucumber
- white as a sheet
- blind as a bat

... or any other comparison that your reader will have read many times before.

Now try this

Choose **one** of these exam-style questions.

Component 1:

> The Ideal Home. **(40 marks)**

Component 2:

> **B2** Your local newspaper has published an article suggesting that young people grow up too fast.
> You have decided to write to the newspaper giving your views on this subject. You could write in favour or against the view given in the newspaper.
> **Write a thoughtful article for the newspaper giving your views. (20 marks)**

Write **three** short extracts from your chosen task. Use **one** of the language techniques above in each task.

Had a look ☐ Nearly there ☐ Nailed it! ☐

Using the senses

Using **the five senses** is one of the techniques you can use to **develop** your ideas and **engage** the reader, particularly in your **creative prose writing**. You might also use the senses in some transactional writing, for example a travel review.

The five senses

The five senses are: **sight**, **sound**, **touch**, **taste** and **smell**. Use the five senses (not just sight):

- when you describe a place or an experience
- to make your descriptions vivid
- to engage the reader
- to help the reader to imagine they are there
- to help your writing to stand out.

This sentence uses descriptive language to create an image:

> He could see that the fridge was crammed to the top with mouldy, stinking food that looked as if it was at least two years past its sell-by date.

Try to **show, not tell.** A paragraph starting 'he saw', followed by 'then he smelt' and 'later he touched' is unlikely to engage the reader.

These carefully chosen adjectives **show** the reader.

This **tells** the reader with the words 'he could see'.

Careful choice of verbs and descriptive detail shows rather than tells the reader about what is seen and felt.

An adverb is used to intensify this use of the sense of sight.

Clever use of sense of smell avoids telling the reader 'The fridge smelled very bad'.

Notice how this extract is more engaging and powerful because the senses of smell and touch are used to add detail.

> He recoiled from the fridge door as the fumes assaulted his nostrils. Had somebody actually died in there? Peering cautiously in it was obvious that every corner was crammed with mouldy, stinking food that looked as if it was at least two years past its sell-by date. His fingers brushed against something soft and furry buried in the door. The source of the fumes – something that hadn't actually been milk since the last century.

Now try this

This plan describes a kitchen. Produce a quickly sketched plan for **another** setting of your choice. It could be a room or somewhere outside.

Include the five senses in your planning:

Planning the five senses

This plan also includes use of similes, metaphor and personification. These techniques work very well together with the five senses to build up descriptions of settings.

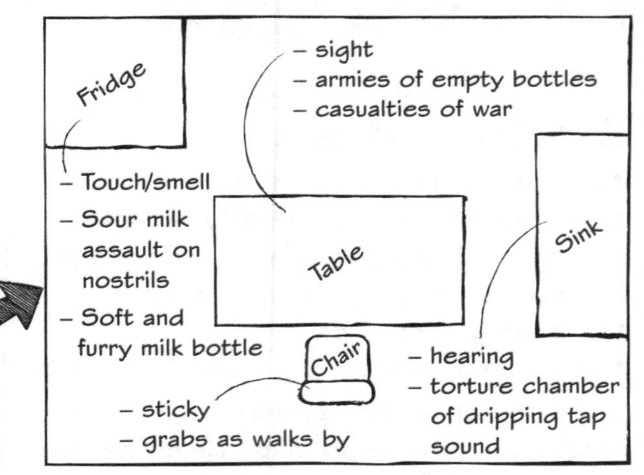

Narrative voice

In **Component 1: Section B – Writing**, you might need to decide on the **viewpoint** of your **creative prose writing**. This is called the **narrative voice**.

See page 22 for more about narrative voice

First-person narrative

This is a narrative written in the first person ('I').

Told by an 'I' – the 'I' can be the main character or a less important character who is witnessing events

Effective in giving a sense of closeness to the character

Allows the story to be told in the character's distinctive voice and language

I crashed the car when she told me. It was such an ordinary day – we were just in the car park at the shopping centre, waiting for a space to become free.

'Julie, I'm getting married.' Francesca paused for no more than one beat of my heart. 'To Michael.'

My heart banged and blood rushed through my ears as I fought for breath. With a sickening crunch the car slammed into a post, hurtling us both into our seatbelts, leaving us winded and speechless. Looking over at the passenger seat, I have to admit that I was sorry she was still breathing!

Third-person narrative

This is a narrative written in the third person. The narrator is **not** one of the characters in the story.

Characters are referred to by name or as 'he' or 'she'.

The narrator can see into any character's mind and reveal their thoughts and feelings to the reader.

An 'omniscient' (all-knowing) third-person narrator knows everything about all the characters and events.

Julie crashed the car when she heard the news. It had started as just an ordinary day for her and when the bombshell was dropped she was drumming her fingers on the steering wheel, waiting for a space to become free. Francesca said it casually, 'I'm getting married.' She paused for no more than a split second, anxious to get the news out before she lost her nerve. 'To Michael.'

The car slammed into the post with a sickening crunch, hurtling both women into their seatbelts, leaving them winded and speechless. Francesca was rigid with fear – why had she told her now? Julie was impulsive at the best of times...

Now try this

Read the student answers above. Identify **two** advantages and **two** disadvantages of each narrative voice.

Remember to:
- check if the exam paper tells you which narrative voice to use
- decide which narrative voice you will write in, if you are given the choice
- stick to the narrative voice you choose throughout your answer.

Had a look ☐ Nearly there ☐ Nailed it! ☐

Putting it into practice

For **Component 2: Section B – Writing** you will need to show you can use language to write effectively for **different audiences and purposes**. Look at the exam-style question below and read the extracts from two students' answers.

Worked example

Your local newspaper has published an article suggesting that families with young children should not be allowed to own dogs.

You have decided to write a letter to the newspaper giving your views. You could choose either to agree with the view in the article, or disagree with the view.

Write a formal letter to the newspaper setting out your views. (20 marks)

Using language in transactional writing

In each of your writing tasks you should:

- ✓ **annotate** the question to highlight the **form, audience and purpose**
- ✓ choose **language** that is appropriate for the **audience and purpose**
- ✓ choose **language techniques** with care and for **impact**

In this example, you need to **persuade** the audience of your own point of view and **argue against** the other point of view.

Sample answer

Why do parents think that letting their kids have a dog is a good idea?

This week we heard about another kid being bitten in his own home by the family pet. The baby did not die, but will be scarred for life. And what will be the effect of being bitten by an animal he loved?

In my own family, our pets have caused some problems for us all…

✓ Rhetorical questions set out argument at start and keep the reader engaged

✗ Language too informal for form, audience and purpose

✓ Use of evidence to support argument

✗ Unimaginative vocabulary means the argument is less persuasive

Improved sample answer

Why do parents feel children's lives will be enhanced by dog ownership? For all of the upsides – and I appreciate that dogs can become a real part of the family – attacks by man's best friend have increased by 40% in the last year alone.

Yet again this week, we heard about another toddler being savaged in his own home by the family pet. Luckily, the baby did not die, but he will carry the scars for the rest of his life. And what about the consequences of being brutally mauled by a beloved and trusted member of the family?

Thankfully, my own family has not suffered to that extreme degree.

✓ Rhetorical question, with the appropriately formal language 'children', indicates the argument will be serious and factual.

✓ Statistics supply evidence in the opening paragraph to create trustworthy tone.

✓ A wide range of (correctly spelled) ambitious vocabulary is used for emotive effect.

See pages 53 and 58 for reminders about writing to argue and persuade, and writing letters

In this sample answer, emotive words and phrases are used to shock, which strengthens the argument.

Now try this

Finish the third paragraph of the Improved sample answer opposite and then complete the letter. Remember to include a counter-argument and use adverbials to link your key points and paragraphs.

Putting it into practice

For **Component 1: Section B – Writing** you will need to show you can use language effectively in **creative prose writing**. Look at the exam-style question below and read the extracts from two students' answers.

Worked example

Write about a time when you made a mistake. **(40 marks)**

Language choice

In each of your writing tasks you should:

- ✓ choose language appropriate to your audience
- ✓ make ambitious and effective vocabulary choices to engage your reader
- ✓ use a range of language techniques.

Sample answer

The worst mistake I ever made was jumping out of a tree. I was down the park with my friends and they dared me to climb this really tall tree. I was about eight. So I climbed up the tree. I got about a metre up and it felt like I was nearly at the sky. I looked down and realised I hadn't got very far and they were all laughing and shouting and encouraging me to go higher. So I carried on climbing. I went up another metre or so. By now I was really scared.

✗ Opening unimaginative and does not create a narrative tone

✗ Language choice too informal and unimaginative

✗ Limited description, and unambitious vocabulary choice

✓ Effective use of figurative language

Note that although there is some limited (but effective) language choice here, there are also missed opportunities to use really effective language (as you can see in the final sentence).

Improved sample answer

My aunt had come to stay. She was a stern, grey-faced woman with eyes that could turn you to stone. When she entered a room, an arctic cold crept through the air, freezing you instantly into silence. The only thing that would make my aunt crack her face and bring out a smile was cake. She loved it. Cream cake, chocolate cake, fruit cake, any cake would bring a rosy glow to her cheeks and her long, sharpened teeth out from between her grey lips. And that was where the trouble started.

✓ Engaging vocabulary choice

✓ Effective use of language devices:

- metaphor
- personification
- list

Notice how this language choice shows humour as well as being effective.

Now try this

Write the **first two** paragraphs of your answer to the exam-style question above.

Remember to choose and use:

- language appropriate to your audience
- language for effect
- a range of ambitious vocabulary and language features.

Had a look ☐ Nearly there ☐ Nailed it! ☐

Sentence variety 1

Using a range of **different sentence types** in your **transactional writing** and your **creative prose writing** can help you to keep your readers engaged.

Engaging the reader

Writing for young children uses a limited range of sentence types:

> Penny went out of the house.
> It was raining.
> Soon she was soaked.
> Penny turned around and went home again.

Effective writing for adults uses a variety of sentence types to hold the reader's interest.

Sentence types

These are the basic types of sentence:

- single-clause
- multi-clause
- minor.

To remind yourself which is which, look back at page 28. You will need to use all of these types of sentence in your writing.

Multi-clause sentences

Multi-clause sentences can help you to keep your readers engaged with your ideas. These are the main types.

Sentences using a subordinate clause

- This is additional information which is added to the main clause using conjunctions such as: because, although, if, since.
- The subordinate clause is dependent on the main clause because it doesn't make sense without it.

Subordinate clause — Main clause

> Before I went out, I locked all the doors.

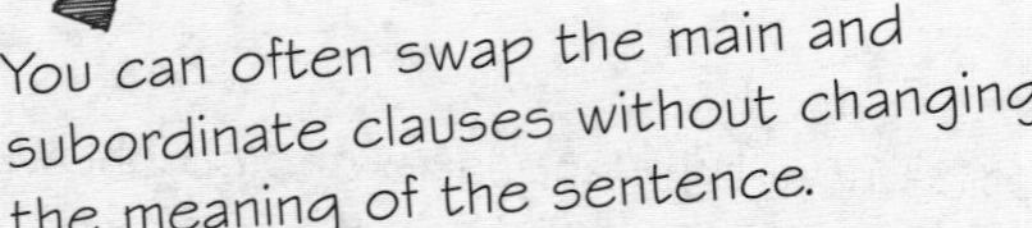

You can often swap the main and subordinate clauses without changing the meaning of the sentence.

Sentences using a coordinate clause

If neither clause is dependent on the other, then the clauses are coordinate. Coordinate clauses use conjunctions such as: and, but, or.

Main clause — These clauses are an equal pair.

> I checked that the windows were shut and I locked the front door.

Sentences using a relative clause

This is where additional information is introduced use a **relative pronoun**, such as: that, where, which, whose, who, when.

Main clause — Relative clause, separated from the main clause with commas

> The neighbour, who I've never liked, waved as I walked down the front path.

Now try this

Write the opening paragraph for this **Component 1 creative prose writing** exam-style question:

My Room.	**(40 marks)**

Aim to use at least one of:

- a single-clause sentence
- a multi-clause sentence (subordinate clause)
- a multi-clause sentence (coordinate clause)
- a multi-clause sentence (relative clause)
- a minor sentence.

Sentence variety 2

Thinking about the **first word** of your sentences can help you **add interest** to your **transactional writing** and your **creative prose writing**.

First words

Developing writers often start their sentences in similar ways. Try to start your sentences in different ways to engage your reader. You can start with any of these.

Type of word	Examples
A pronoun I, you, he, she, it, we, they, my, your	I turned and started.
An article a, an, the	The glass had disappeared.
A preposition above, behind, between, near, with, etc.	Above me, I heard footsteps.
An -ing word (or present participle) running, hurrying, crawling, smiling, etc.	Edging silently to the door, I went to the stairs and listened.
An adjective slow, quiet, huge, violent, etc.	Sharp, prickling pains crept from my fingertips to my hair.
An adverb alarmingly, painfully, happily, etc.	Gingerly, I put my foot on the first stair.
A conjunction (subordinate clause + main clause) if, although, because, when, while, etc.	Although I knew I was in an empty house, I could not help thinking that I was not alone.

Getting it right

Make your writing more engaging by:

- using a variety of different types of sentence opener
- using a variety of sentence types.

Now try this

Using at least five of the above styles of sentence opener, write the opening of an answer to this **Component 1 creative prose writing** exam-style question:

My first day at school. **(40 marks)**

Sentences for different effects

Structuring your sentences in different ways can achieve different effects. For example, you can vary your sentence structure in a piece of transactional writing to emphasise an argument, or in your creative prose writing to achieve a particular mood.

Longer sentences

Use longer, **multi-clause** sentences to deliver more information sharply and concisely. You can add information using one or more subordinate clauses, as the example opposite shows.

Beware: if you overload a sentence with too much information, spread over a number of subordinate clauses, you could lose your reader's attention.

Main clause — Relative clause

The house, which I had never visited before, seemed strangely familiar.

Notice how the clauses have been separated with commas.

The long and the short

Short, punchy, **single-clause** sentences can be particularly effective: they add impact to an argument, and surprise or tension to a description. Look at the contrast opposite.

Short, single-clause sentences are particularly effective when they follow a longer multi-clause sentence.

Long sentence to contrast with a short sentence to surprise.

Some people believe in leaping out of bed as the sun is rising and settling down to an hour's revision before breakfast, then a couple of hours' more revision before a short jog to revive the brain and another couple of hours' revision before lunchtime. I do not.

In order of importance

You can structure your sentences for emphasis. Important information is usually placed at the end of a sentence.

Arrange your sentences so that the point you want to emphasise comes at the end.

- This sentence gives more emphasis to the revision than the exams because it comes at the end of the sentence:

The final insult is that the dreaded exams come after all that revision.

- This sentence emphasises the dreaded exams, giving the sentence more impact:

The final insult is that after all that revision come the dreaded exams.

Now try this

Write **one** or **two** paragraphs in response to this **Component 2** exam-style question.

Aim to include:
- a long sentence followed by a short sentence
- a sentence structured to leave the important information until the end.

B1 Your school is keen to increase participation in after-school sports clubs.

Write a report for the Headteacher suggesting ways that this could be done.

You could include:
- examples of sports that could be offered
- your ideas about how to attract students to the clubs. **(20 marks)**

Putting it into practice

For **both components** you will need to show you can vary your sentences for effect. Look at the **Component 2** exam-style question below and read the extracts from two students' answers.

Worked example

B2 Many people believe that it is important to follow fashion and look good.

You have decided to write an article for a teenage magazine giving your views. You could write in favour of this belief or against it.

Write a lively magazine article giving your views. (20 marks)

Sentence variety

In each of the writing tasks you should:

- ✓ use a range of sentence structures
- ✓ start your sentences in different ways
- ✓ structure your sentences for effect.

Sample answer

Fashion is important because people judge you on how you look, even though you shouldn't it's difficult not to. Fashion can also be fun because shopping and choosing clothes and seeing what your friends are wearing is really enjoyable. Fashion is also something to talk about and do with your friends because if all your friends are in fashion and like the same fashion then you can swap clothes and tell them how they look.

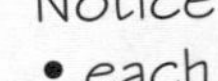

Notice that:

- each sentence starts in the same way
- each sentence follows the same structure
- sentences are all long, using multiple clauses.

To improve your answer you should add variety.

✗ Vocabulary is frequently repeated.

✗ A limited range of adverbials creates repetitive vocabulary and sentence structure.

Improved sample answer

We all judge a book by its cover. We don't mean to but we do. But should we? Even if we don't want to judge others, we expect others to judge us. We primp, preen and polish ourselves for hours, preparing ourselves to be seen by the world. How disappointing would it be if, after all that effort, no one bothered to look and make the right judgement? The truth is that, no matter how much we might not want appearances to matter, they do. They matter very much.

Notice how this answer starts with:

- two short sentences to create an emphatic opening
- a rhetorical question that engages the reader
- a neatly structured sentence.

✓ A second rhetorical question further engages reader.

✓ Long sentence, followed by powerful short sentence, further emphasised with repetition to engage the reader.

Now try this

Write the **first two** paragraphs of your answer to the exam-style question above.

Remember to:

- use a range of sentence types and lengths
- start sentences in a variety of ways
- structure sentences for effect.

Had a look ☐ Nearly there ☐ Nailed it! ☐

Ending a sentence

In **both components** your writing will be marked for the quality of your **punctuation**. Make sure you start each sentence with a **capital letter**. End each sentence with a **full stop, an exclamation mark or a question mark**.

Check your full stops

Most students know that a sentence should start with a capital letter and end with a full stop. However, mistakes are often made. The most common error is using a comma to join two sentences instead of a full stop to separate them. This is called a **comma splice**.

Avoiding the comma splice

When you want to tell the reader two pieces of information you can do two things.

Separate them with a full stop:

> Puppies are small and cuddly. People do not seem to realise that they will soon grow.

Join them with a conjunction:

> Puppies are small and cuddly **but** people do not seem to realise that they will soon grow.

You **cannot** join them with a comma:

> Puppies are small and cuddly, people do not seem to realise that they will soon grow.

Question marks

Always check you have actually put a question mark at the end of a question – especially if it is a rhetorical question.

Exclamation marks

Be **very** careful in your use of exclamation marks. Follow these golden rules:

- Only use an exclamation mark for a real exclamation, e.g. 'Thank goodness!' he cried.
- Use them very sparingly. Don't scatter them randomly throughout your writing.
- Never use two or more exclamation marks in a row.

Now try this

Rewrite this student's answer, removing all the comma splices. Try to do this in three different ways by:

- adding conjunctions
- restructuring some of the sentences
- replacing the comma splices with full stops.

> Remember that you do not use a comma to join two pieces of information in a sentence. Use a full stop to separate them, or a conjunction to join them.

> I was born in the countryside, I grew up surrounded by the sounds and smells of the natural world, when I was ten we moved to the city; it was a confusing, fast-paced, deafening environment that I found hard to love. It was such a big change, it came as quite a shock to my system, worst of all I had to leave all my friends behind and try to make new ones in this strange, unfamiliar place. I was lonely, convinced I would never feel at home, before a year had passed I had the best friend anyone could wish for.

Commas

It is very important that you feel confident using **commas**, as you will need to use them to create effective multi-clause sentences and **lists**.

Also see page 28 for a reminder about sentence types

Commas and subordinate clauses

In a multi-clause sentence, the main clause and the subordinate clause can usually be swapped around without changing the meaning of the sentence:

I meet new people (main clause)
wherever I go. (subordinate clause)

If you begin a multi-clause sentence with the main clause, there is no need for a comma to separate the clauses.

Wherever I go, (subordinate clause)
I meet new people. (main clause)

If you begin a multi-clause sentence with the subordinate clause, use a comma to separate it from the main clause.

Commas and relative clauses

You can add a relative clause to a sentence, giving additional information linked with one of these relative pronouns:

- that
- whose
- where
- who
- which
- when.

You should always separate the relative clause from the main clause with commas.

Main clause — Relative clause

The house, which I had never visited before, seemed strangely familiar.

Notice how the clauses have been separated with commas.

Commas in a list

If you are writing a list, add a comma after each word or phrase – apart from the words or phrases that are linked using and.

- Use commas in lists of adjectives:

He was tall, smartly dressed and elegant.

Comma here to separate two items in a list.

No comma here because they are linked with and.

- Use commas in lists of phrases:

There was mud on the floor, mud on the walls, mud on the windows and mud on the ceiling.

Now try this

Look at this **Component 1 creative prose writing** exam-style question:

The School Trip. **(40 marks)**

Write **three** to **five** sentences, using commas correctly to separate:

- items in a list
- a main and subordinate clause
- a main and relative clause.

End your sentences correctly. Avoid using a **comma splice**.

Apostrophes and speech punctuation

Missing or incorrect **apostrophes** and **speech punctuation** are common errors. You may need to use dialogue in **both components**, so make sure you know how to avoid mistakes.

Apostrophes in contractions

When two words are shortened or abbreviated, some letters are missed out or omitted. You should use an apostrophe to show where these letters are missing:

cannot → **can't**
do not → **don't**
I will → **I'll**
let us → **let's**

Abbreviations such as **don't** and **can't** are more informal than the full, unabbreviated versions. Think about your audience when deciding which to use.

Apostrophes of possession

Apostrophes can be used to show that something or someone belongs to someone or something else.

- The boy's hands …
- Betty's sister …
- The dog's collar …
- The school's head teacher …

Note that if the word to which you are adding the apostrophe ends in s you can just add the apostrophe after the s:

The teachers' voices

Mrs Roberts' book

Note that this is a plural: there is more than one teacher.

You can also, when a name ends in s, add an apostrophe and another s.

Mrs Roberts's book

Speech punctuation

- Use speech marks to enclose the words that are spoken.
- Start the speech with a capital letter.
- There is always a punctuation mark just before the closing speech marks.
- Use a comma if you are adding who is speaking …
- … followed by a lower case letter immediately after the closing speech marks.
- Use a full stop if you are not adding who is speaking.

'Mum, can I have some sweets?' begged Aran.

'It's nearly dinner time,' his mother replied.

'Mum, I want some sweets.'

'I've just told you,' said his mother patiently.

Avoid too much dialogue in creative prose writing. Focus on full paragraphs of prose to show you understand sentence structures.

Now try this

There are **13** punctuation errors in this student's writing. Copy and correct it.

'theres nothing I can do said Garys dad.
'are you sure,' Replied Gary.
'idont know what you mean.' Said his dad.
'i think you do'

Colons, semi-colons, dashes, brackets and ellipses

Punctuation can help you develop your ideas and express yourself clearly.

Semi-colons

You can **link two connected ideas** with a semi-colon instead of a conjunction.

For example, you could write:

> Education is a privilege and it should be treasured.

Or you could write:

> Education is a privilege; it should be treasured.

Dashes and brackets

These can be used to **add** extra, but not entirely necessary, information to a sentence. Before using brackets or dashes, ask yourself: Is this important information? Or would my writing be better without it?

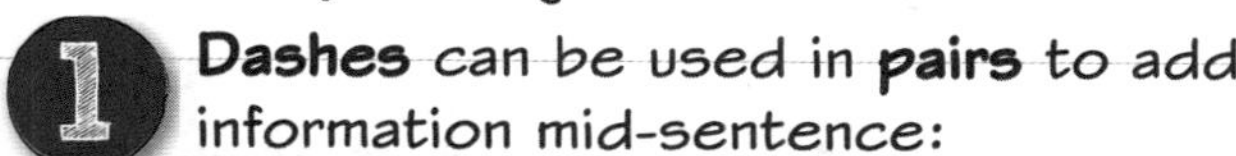

1 **Dashes** can be used in **pairs** to add information mid-sentence:

> Several years ago – though I can't remember exactly when – my sister moved to Scotland.

2 **Single dashes** can be used at the end of a sentence, to suggest a pause before an afterthought:

> I'm sure there was a reason – but no one ever told me what it was.

3 **Brackets** must be used in **pairs**:

> The house (which my mother hated) was near the sea.

Colons

Use a colon to **introduce an example**:

> Students have two choices: work hard or fail.

Or to **introduce a list**:

> You will need: a pen, a pencil, a ruler and an eraser.

Or to **introduce an explanation**:

> English is my favourite subject: I love creative writing.

Ellipses

You can use an ellipsis in **dialogue** to suggest a **dramatic pause** or to show someone falling into **silence**:

> 'I don't know where I...'
> He looked mystified.

> 'And the winner is...'

Using an ellipsis to suggest tension in descriptive writing can seem clichéd. Instead, create tension through your choice of language and sentence structure:

✗
> He opened the door and realised to his horror that the room was completely empty...

✓
> He opened the door. The room was completely empty.

Now try this

Answer the following questions using the information on this page.

1 What punctuation could you use to introduce an explanation?

2 What could you use instead of a conjunction to link two connected ideas?

3 When might you use a pair of dashes?

Putting it into practice

For **both components** you will need to show you can use a range of punctuation accurately. Look at the **Component 2** exam-style question below and read the extracts from two students' answers.

Worked example

B1 Your school magazine is holding a writing competition with the title 'I couldn't live without...'.

Write your entry as an informative article, explaining what you couldn't live without and why it is important to you. (20 marks)

You could write about:

- a hobby
- a pet
- a person.

Punctuation

In each of the writing tasks you need to show you can:

- ✓ punctuate accurately
- ✓ use a full range of punctuation
- ✓ use punctuation effectively to express yourself clearly.

Sample answer

I could'nt live without football, its something I've always loved. I love playing it and watching it whether its a few friends having a kickabout at lunchtime or an FA Cup final on the telly. There are lots of reasons it means so much to me. One is that my dad loves football so its something we have in common. He does'nt play football but we can spend hours talking about it, who scored, who didnt score who should be playing and who should be dropped.

- ✗ Incorrectly placed apostrophes.
- ✗ Comma splice. This should either be a semi-colon or a full stop followed by a new sentence.
- ✗ Missing apostrophe.
- ✗ Missed opportunity for a colon to introduce a list.
- ✗ Missing comma separating items in a list.

Note that the use of full stops in the first answer is **generally** accurate.

Improved sample answer

The only thing which I cannot imagine ever being without is my dog. She doesn't bark, she doesn't growl, she doesn't jump up; she's perfect in every way. Just the sight of her floppy ears, her wagging tail and her shiny black eyes can put a smile on my face. I remember when I got her: it was my ninth birthday, a day I will always remember. I opened all my presents – none of which I can remember now – and my mum said she had one more surprise for me. She brought in a small cardboard box.

The full stops in the improved answer are **completely** accurate.

- ✓ Correct use of apostrophe.
- ✓ Commas, semi-colons and colons are all used accurately. Notice how the commas separate items in a list, the colon is used to introduce an explanation, and the semi-colon acts like a full stop.

Dashes like these are used to add additional information.

Now try this

Write the first paragraph of your answer to the above exam-style question. Aim to use a range of punctuation accurately, including commas, apostrophes, colons and semi-colons.

Always remember to check your punctuation – especially full stops – for accuracy.

Common spelling errors 1

For **both components** you will need to show you can spell correctly. There are some spelling mistakes that occur again and again in students' exam responses. Learn how to avoid making them.

Would have, could have, should have

Students often use **would of** or **should of** or **could of** when they should use **would have**, **should have**, or **could have.** For example:

✗ Global warming could of been prevented. We should of started thinking more carefully about the environment long ago.

This is what should have been written:
could **have** ✓ should **have** ✓

Our, are

Students often confuse *our* and *are*:

- **our** means *belonging to us*
- **are** is from the verb *to be.*

 We should always look after are bodies. They our precious.

This is what should have been written:
our bodies ✓ **are** precious ✓

There, their, they're

Make sure you learn these spellings:

- **their** means belonging to **them**
- **there** is used to describe the position of something **(It's over there)** and in the phrases **There is** or **There are**
- **they're** is an abbreviation of **they are**.

 Their were three people at the table, all eating there dinner.

 ~~Their~~ There were three people at the table, all eating ~~there~~ their dinner.

Affect, effect

One of these is a verb, and the other a noun:
affect is a verb
effect is usually used as a noun.
So, for example, you may have been **affected** by a problem. But the problem had an **effect** on you. If the word has got **an** or **the** in front of it, it's a noun, so it's spelt **effect**.

Remember: don't be afraid to use an effective word because you're not sure about the spelling.

-ly or -ley?

When you add -ly to a word, make sure you don't swap the 'l' and the 'e':

definite + ly = definitely

bravley ✗ bravely ✓
safley ✗ safely ✓
rudley ✗ rudely ✓

There are **very few** words which end in -ley. Learn these examples: alley, medley, trolley, valley.

Its or it's?

It's is an abbreviation of **it is. Its** means belonging to **it**.

✗ Its the end of it's life.

✓ ~~Its~~ It's the end of ~~it's~~ its life.

Now try this

Look back at the last five pieces of writing you have completed. Have you made any of these common spelling errors? If so, correct them.

Had a look ☐ Nearly there ☐ Nailed it! ☐

Common spelling errors 2

Your and you're

Learn the difference between these two words:

- **your** means **belonging to you**
- **you're** is an abbreviation of **you are.**

✗ Your having the time of you're life.

✓ ~~Your~~ You're having the time of ~~you're~~ your life.

Remember: **A lot** is two words. **Alot of people love chocolate** is wrong, but **A lot of people love chocolate** is correct.

We're, wear, were and where

Make sure you are familiar with each of these:

- **we're** is an abbreviation of **we are**
- **wear** is a verb referring to clothing – e.g. **What are you wearing tonight?**
- **were** is the past tense of are – e.g. **they are, they were**
- **where** is a question word referring to place – e.g. **Where are we going?**

✗ Wear we're you? Were leaving now.

~~Wear we're~~ Where were you? ~~Were~~ We're leaving now.

Two, too, to

Getting these words wrong is quite a common error:

- **to** indicates place, direction or position – e.g. **I went to Spain.**
- **too** means **also** or an **excessive amount** – e.g. **I went too far.**
- **two** is a number.

✗ It's to difficult to get too the highest level.

✓ It's ~~to~~ too difficult to get ~~too~~ to the highest level.

Of, off

The easiest way to remember the difference is by listening to the sound of the word you want to use:

- **of** is pronounced ov
- **off** rhymes with cough.

✗ He jumped of the top off the wall.

✓ He jumped ~~of~~ off the top ~~off~~ of the wall.

Past, passed

Aim to get these two right:

- **passed** is the past tense of the verb to pass – e.g. **He passed all his GCSEs.**
- **past** refers to time that has gone by, or *position* – e.g. **That's all in the past; He ran past the school.**

✗ She past out at ten passed six.

✓ She ~~past~~ passed out at ten ~~passed~~ past six.

Who's and whose

Whose is a question word referring to belonging, e.g. **Whose book is this?**

Who's is an abbreviation of **who is.**

✗ Whose wearing who's coat?

✓ ~~Whose~~ Who's wearing ~~who's~~ whose coat?

Now try this

There are **nine** spelling errors in this student's writing. Copy and correct it.

I saw Annabel walk passed wearing you're shoes. She was carrying you're bag to. I don't know who's coat she had on but it had too stripes across the back. She stopped and took it of. I don't know were she was going or what she was up two. It was very strange.

Common spelling errors 3

Some of the most frequently misspelt words are listed below. Make sure you learn how to spell these words properly.

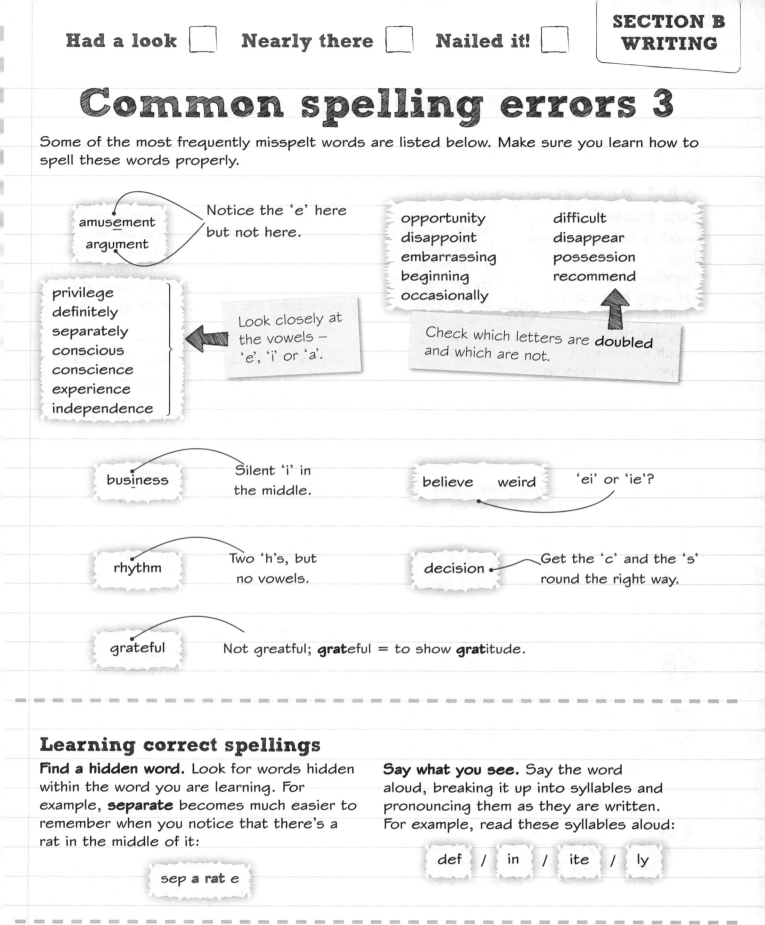

amusement
argument

Notice the 'e' here but not here.

opportunity
disappoint
embarrassing
beginning
occasionally
difficult
disappear
possession
recommend

Check which letters are **doubled** and which are not.

privilege
definitely
separately
conscious
conscience
experience
independence

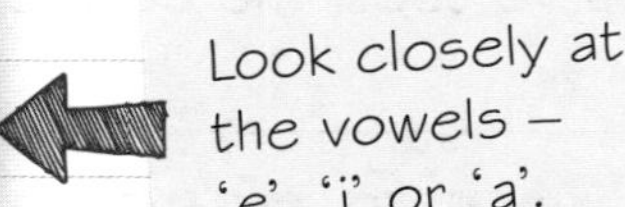

Look closely at the vowels – 'e', 'i' or 'a'.

business – Silent 'i' in the middle.

believe weird – 'ei' or 'ie'?

rhythm – Two 'h's, but no vowels.

decision – Get the 'c' and the 's' round the right way.

grateful – Not greatful; **grat**eful = to show **grat**itude.

Learning correct spellings

Find a hidden word. Look for words hidden within the word you are learning. For example, **separate** becomes much easier to remember when you notice that there's a rat in the middle of it:

sep **a rat** e

Say what you see. Say the word aloud, breaking it up into syllables and pronouncing them as they are written. For example, read these syllables aloud:

def / in / ite / ly

Now try this

Test yourself on these spellings. Learn any that you get wrong, then you could ask a friend or family member to re-test you.

Had a look ☐ Nearly there ☐ Nailed it! ☐

Proofreading

For **both components** it is essential that you leave time at the end of the exam to **check your work**. It could make all the difference.

What kinds of mistakes do you make?

Here's a list of common errors:

- spelling mistakes
- missing or incorrect punctuation
- grammatical errors such as misused, repeated or missing words.

Most people make **all three** kinds of mistakes, especially when they are writing in a hurry.

Ideally, you should check your work through three times:

- once for spelling
- once for punctuation
- once to check it makes clear sense, with no misused, repeated or missing words.

You **will** have made mistakes. Aim to find **five or more** in each of your answers.

Alarm bells

Train your proofreading brain to ring an alarm bell whenever you come across their, there, its, it's or any one of the common spelling errors that everyone makes. When the alarm rings, **stop!** Double check that you've used the correct spelling.

How to check your spelling

If you know you've spelt a word incorrectly, but you're not sure of the correct spelling, try it three or four different ways in the margin. Pick the one that looks right:

seperatly	separetly
separately ✓	separatley

Reading your work backwards – from bottom to top, right to left – stops you thinking about the meaning of your writing and makes you focus on spelling.

Checking for sense: tips

1. When you are checking for sense, try to read 'aloud inside your head' imagining you can hear your voice.
2. Remember to leave time to check your work at the end of the exam. If you check each answer as soon as you've finished writing it, you'll see what you **think** you wrote, not what you **actually** wrote.
3. If you come across a sentence that is clumsy, doesn't make sense, or both... cross it out and try expressing it in a different way.

Putting it right

Accurate writing achieves higher marks than neat writing. So, if you find a mistake – whether it's a word, a sentence, or a whole paragraph – **cross it out**. Put **one neat line** through the mistake and add your correction by:

- using one of these ⁁ ~~to make a mistake~~ (to guide the reader)
- or by using an asterisk.*

* To tell the reader to read this bit next.

If you forget to start a new paragraph, use // to mark where one paragraph ends and the next one begins.

Now try this

Look over five pieces of writing you have produced recently. How many mistakes can you find?

Putting it into practice

For **both components** your writing needs to be as **accurate** as possible. You need to check your work for **errors** in **spelling**, **punctuation** and **grammar**. Look at the **Component 2** exam-style question below and read the extracts from two students' answers.

Worked example

B1 Your local newspaper recently published an article arguing that all teenagers should have a part-time job to teach them the value of money.

You have decided to write a letter to the editor in reply to this article. You can write either for or against what is said in the article.

Write a letter to the newspaper giving your views. **(10 marks)**

Proofreading

For all your writing tasks you should:

- ✓ spend about 3–5 minutes carefully checking your work
- ✓ correct any spelling errors
- ✓ correct any punctuation errors
- ✓ ensure your writing makes clear sense and is legible.

Finding and changing errors could really improve your answer.

Sample answer

Everyone says GCSEs have got easyer but they dont realise how difficult they are and how how much work we have to do at school. There just isn't time to do all the school work and have a part-time job, we need some to rest and and enjoy ourselves. On an avarage day I go to school for six hours, get home and do an hour or two of homework. I could go out to work in the evenings but Id get home late and be realy tired at school the next day which would make it realy dificult to concentrate at school the next day.

Make sure you spend some time checking your answers. The second sentence:

- is clumsily written
- has errors
- is not clear in its meaning.

✗ Spelling errors

✗ Punctuation errors

Improved sample answer

Working for my money has certainly taught me its value. For example, when I was younger and wanted to buy something, I had to pester my mum.* Now, because I've e~~r~~arned my money, ~~I can buy what I want. Because of that I always make sure I know I want what I'm buying.~~ I make very sure I'm not wasting my money on something I ~~dont~~ → don't really need.

* Usually, once I'd got it, I would realise that I didn't really want it anymore.

✓ Spelling and punctuation errors both corrected.

✓ The additional explanation effectively reinforces the argument.

It's fine to cross out clumsy writing and add in something that is easier to read and understand.

Now try this

Look back at a piece of writing you have completed recently. Check it **three** times, looking for:

- sentences that are clumsily written or unclear
- missing or repeated words
- spelling mistakes
- punctuation errors.

Aim to find at least **five** mistakes and correct them.

EXTRACTS

Cut along the dotted lines and staple the texts together to make your own handy anthology. Make sure you keep it safe with your Revision Guide.

EXTRACT 1 – REBECCA

The novel from which this extract is taken opens with the narrator's description of a dream she has had. Manderley is a house she once lived in.

Last night I dreamt I went to Manderley again. It seemed to me I stood by the iron gate leading to the drive, and for a while I could not enter, for the way was barred to me. There was a padlock and a chain upon the gate. I called in my dream to the lodge-keeper, and had no answer, and peering closer through the rusted spokes of the gate I saw that the lodge was uninhabited.

No smoke came from the chimney, and the little lattice windows gaped forlorn. Then, like all dreamers, I was possessed of a sudden with supernatural powers and passed like a spirit through the barrier before me. The drive wound away in front of me, twisting and turning as it had always done, but as I advanced I was aware that a change had come upon it; it was narrow and unkept, not the drive that we had known. At first I was puzzled and did not understand, and it was only when I bent my head to avoid the low swinging branch of a tree that I realized what had happened. Nature had come into her own again and, little by little, in her stealthy, insidious way had encroached upon the drive with long, tenacious fingers. The woods, always a menace even in the past, had triumphed in the end. They crowded, dark and uncontrolled, to the borders of the drive. The beeches with white, naked limbs leant close to one another, their branches intermingled in a strange embrace, making a vault above my head like the archway of a church. And there were other trees as well, trees that I did not recognize, squat oaks and tortured elms that straggled cheek by jowl with the beeches, and had thrust themselves out of the quiet earth, along with monster shrubs and plants, none of which I remembered.

The drive was a ribbon now, a thread of its former self, with gravel surface gone, and choked with grass and moss. The trees had thrown out low branches, making an impediment to progress; the gnarled roots looked like skeleton claws. Scattered here and again amongst this jungle growth I would recognize shrubs that had been landmarks in our time, things of culture and grace, hydrangeas whose blue heads had been famous. No hand had checked their progress, and they had gone native now, rearing to monster height without a bloom, black and ugly as the nameless parasites that grew beside them.

On and on, now east now west, wound the poor thread that once had been our drive. Sometimes I thought it lost, but it appeared again, beneath a fallen tree perhaps, or struggling on the other side of a muddied ditch created by the winter rains. I had not thought the way so long. Surely the miles had multiplied, even as the trees had done, and this path led but to a labyrinth, some choked wilderness, and not to the house at all. I came upon it suddenly; the approach masked by the unnatural growth of a vast shrub that spread in all directions, and I stood, my heart thumping in my breast, the strange prick of tears behind my eyes.

There was Manderley, our Manderley, secretive and silent as it had always been, the grey stone shining in the moonlight of my dream, the mullioned windows reflecting the green lawns and the terrace. Time could not wreck the perfect symmetry of those walls, nor the site itself, a jewel in the hollow of a hand.

Daphne du Maurier

cheek by jowl, close together
insidious, slow and harmful
inviolate, injury-free
labyrinth, maze
lattice, a pattern of diamond shapes
mullioned windows, windows with vertical bars between the panes of glass

Sometimes you may not be given a glossary. To help work out the meaning of a word, remember to look at the context.

Cut along the dotted lines and staple the texts together to make your own handy anthology. Make sure you keep it safe with your Revision Guide.

EXTRACT 2 – EVERY MAN FOR HIMSELF

The novel from which this extract is taken is set on the ill-fated Titanic. In this passage, the ship is sinking and the passengers are in grave danger.

And now, the moment was almost upon us. The stern began to lift from the water. Guggenheim* and his valet played mountaineers, going hand over hand up the rail. The hymn turned ragged; ceased altogether. The musicians scrambled upwards, the spike of the cello scraping the deck. Clinging to the rung of the ladder I tried to climb to the roof but there was such a sideways slant that I waved like a flag on a pole. I thought I must make a leap for it and turned to look for Hopper*. Something, some inner voice urged me to glance below and I saw Scurra* again, one arm hooked through the rail to steady himself. I raised my hand in greeting – then the water, first slithering, then tumbling, gushed us apart.

As the ship staggered and tipped, a great volume of water flowed in over the submerged bows and tossed me like a cork to the roof. Hopper was there too. My fingers touched some kind of bolt near the ventilation grille and I grabbed it tight. I filled my lungs with air and fixed my eyes on the blurred horizon, determined to hang on until I was sure I could float free rather than be swilled back and forth in a maelstrom. I wouldn't waste my strength in swimming, not yet, for I knew the ship was now my enemy and if I wasn't vigilant would drag me with her to the grave. I waited for the next slithering dip and when it came and the waves rushed in and swept me higher, I released my grip and let myself be carried away, over the tangle of ropes and wires and davits, clear of the rails and out into the darkness. I heard the angry roaring of the dying ship, the deafening cacophony as she stood on end and all her guts tore loose. I choked on soot and cringed beneath the sparks dancing like fire-flies as the forward funnel broke and smashed the sea in two. I thought I saw Hopper's face but one eye was ripped away and he gobbled like a fish on the hook. I was sucked under, as I knew I would be, down, down, and still I waited, waited until the pull slackened – then I struck out with all my strength.

I don't know how long I swam under that lidded sea – time had stopped with my breath – and just as it seemed as if my lungs would burst the blackness paled and I kicked to the surface. I had thought I was entering paradise, for I was alive and about to breathe again, and then I heard the cries of souls in torment and believed myself in hell. Dear God! Those voices! Father… Father… For the love of Christ… Help me, for pity's sake!… Where is my son Some called for their mothers, some on the Lord, some to die quickly, a few to be saved. The lamentations rang through the frosty air and touched the stars; my own mouth opened in a silent howl of grief. The cries went on and on, trembling, lingering – and God forgive me, but I wanted them to end. In all that ghastly night, it was the din of the dying that chilled the most. Presently, the voices grew fainter, ceased – yet still I heard them, as though the drowned called to one another in a ghostly place where none could follow. Then silence fell, and that was the worst sound of all. There was no trace of the *Titanic*. All that remained was a grey veil of vapour drifting above the water.

Gradually I grew accustomed to the darkness and made out a boat some distance away. Summoning up all my strength I swam closer; it was a collapsible, wrong side up and sagging in the sea. I tried to climb on to the gunwale but the occupants gazed through me and offered no assistance; they might have been dead men for all the life in their eyes. Swimming round to the far side, I commandeered a bobbing barrel, and, mounting it like a horse, hand-paddled to the stern and flung myself aboard.

* Guggenheim, Hopper and Scurra are other passengers on the ship.

Beryl Bainbridge

bows, the front end of a ship
davits, small cranes
gunwale, the side of a boat
lamentations, sorrowful cries
maelstrom, a powerful whirlpool
valet, male servant
vapour, mist

EXTRACTS

Cut along the dotted lines and staple the texts together to make your own handy anthology. Make sure you keep it safe with your Revision Guide.

EXTRACT 3 – MY SON'S STORY

The novel from which this extract is taken tells the story of a family in South Africa and their struggle with Apartheid. Here the narrator is describing his early childhood with his family.

We didn't have any particular sense of what we were – my sister and I. I mean, my father made of the circumscription of our life within the areas open to us a charmed circle. Of a kind. I see that I don't want to admit that, now, because it comes to me as a criticism, but the truth is that it did give us some sort of security. He didn't keep from us, in general, the knowledge that there were places we couldn't go, things we couldn't do; but he never tried to expose us to such places, he substituted so many things we could do. My sister had dancing lessons and he taught me to play chess. I was allowed to stay up quite late on Friday night – no school next day – and we'd sit at the table in the kitchen after supper was cleared away, his great black eyes on me, encouraging, serious, crinkling into a smile back in their darkness, while I hesitated to make my move. Every Saturday when we went to town he bought a comic each for me and my sister – not the kind where the vocabulary was limited to onomatopoeic exclamations by supermen (those I borrowed secretly from my pals), but publications from England with stories of brave fighter pilots and King Arthur's Round Table, for me, and romantic fables retold in pictures for my sister.

Why do I say 'he' made the charmed circle in which we lived in innocence? My mother, too, drew it around us. But although they planned everything together and if there was a decision to be made affecting us, or any other matter that could be discussed in front of us, we would see him looking at her (the way he looked at me over the chess board) while he awaited her opinion, I am right in attributing the drawing of the safe circle of our lives, then, to him. It was always as if he knew what she wanted, for him and us, and that she knew he would find the way to articulate the components of daily life accordingly. For what she wanted was, in essence, always what he wanted; and that is not as simple or purely submissive as it sounds. I didn't – don't – pretend to understand how. It was between them, and will not be available to any child of theirs, ever.

What did it matter that the seaside hotels, the beaches, pleasure-grounds with swimming-pools were not for us? We couldn't afford hotels, anyway; a fun fair for the use of our kind came to our area at Easter, the circus came at Christmas, and we picnicked in the no-man's-land of veld between the mine-dumps, where in the summer a spruit ran between the reeds and my father showed us how the weaver birds make their hanging nests. There, on our rug, overseen by nobody, safe from everybody, the drunks next door and the municipality in the town, my father would lay his head in my mother's lap and we children would lie against their sides, under the warmth of their arms. A happy childhood.

But at fifteen you are no longer a child.

Nadine Gordimer

circumscription, boundary, limited area
onomatopoeic exclamations, words that resemble the sound they make e.g. Pow!
veld, a name for open grassland in South Africa
mine-dumps, waste left near a mine
spruit, a South African name for a small stream

Cut along the dotted lines and staple the texts together to make your own handy anthology. Make sure you keep it safe with your Revision Guide.

EXTRACT 4 – ABOUT A BOY

The novel from which this extract is taken is about the unlikely friendship between a boy, Marcus, and a self-centred man called Will. In this passage, they are feeding ducks in the park with their friend Suzie and Suzie's daughter, Megan.

Marcus couldn't believe it. Dead. A dead duck. OK, he'd been *trying* to hit it on the head with a piece of sandwich, but he *tried* to do all sorts of things, and none of them had ever happened before. He'd *tried* to get the highest score on the Stargazer machine in the kebab shop on Hornsey Road – nothing. He'd *tried* to read Nicky's thoughts by staring at the back of his head every maths lesson for a week – nothing. It really annoyed him that the only thing he'd ever achieved was something he hadn't really wanted to do that much in the first place. And anyway, since when did hitting a bird with a sandwich kill it? Kids must spend half their lives throwing things at the ducks in Regent's Park. How come he managed to pick a duck that pathetic? There must have been something wrong with it. It was probably about to die from a heart attack or something; it was just a coincidence. But if it was, nobody would believe him. If there were any witnesses, they'd only have seen the bread hit the duck right on the back of the head, and then seen it keel over. They'd put two and two together and make five, and he'd be imprisoned for a crime he never committed.

Will, Suzie, Megan and Marcus stood on the path at the edge of the lake, staring at the dead body floating in the water.

'There's nothing we can do about it now', said Will, the trendy bloke who was trying to get off with Suzie. 'Just leave it. What's the problem?'

'Well… Supposing someone saw me?'

'D'you think anyone did?'

'I don't know. Maybe. Maybe they said they were going to tell the park-keeper.'

'Maybe someone saw you, or definitely? Maybe they said they were going to get the park-keeper, or definitely?' Marcus didn't like this bloke, so he didn't answer him.

'What's that floating next to it?' Will asked. 'Is that the bread you threw at it?'

Marcus nodded unhappily.

'That's not a sandwich, that's a bloody french loaf. No wonder it keeled over. That would have killed me.'

'Oh, Marcus,' Suzie sighed. 'What were you playing at?'

'Nothing.'

'No, it looks like it,' said Will. Marcus hated him even more. Who did this Will think he was?

'I'm not sure it was me.' He was going to test out his theory. If Suzie didn't believe him, there was no chance the police and judges would.

'How do you mean?'

'I think it must have been ill. I think it was going to die anyway.' Nobody said anything; Will shook his head angrily. Marcus decided this line of defence was a waste of time, even though it was true.

They were staring so hard at the scene of the crime that they didn't notice the park-keeper until he was standing right next to them. Marcus felt his insides turn to mush. This was it.

'One of your ducks has died,' said Will. He made it sound as if it were the saddest thing he'd ever seen. Marcus looked up at him; maybe he didn't hate him after all.

'I was told that you had something to do with it,' said the park-keeper. 'You know that's a criminal offence, don't you?'

'You were told that I had something to do with it?' said Will. 'Me?'

'Maybe not you, but your lad here.'

'You're suggesting that Marcus killed this duck? Marcus *loves* ducks, don't you, Marcus?'

'Yeah. They're my favourite animal. Well, second favourite. After dolphins. They're definitely my favourite bird, though.' This was rubbish because he hated all animals, but he thought it helped.

'I was told he was throwing bloody great french loaves at it.'

'He was, but I've stopped him now. Boys will be boys,' said Will. Marcus hated him again. He might have known he'd grass him up.

'So he killed it?'

'Oh, God no. Sorry, I see what you mean. No, he was throwing bread at the body. I think he was trying to sink it, because Megan here was getting upset.'

The park-keeper looked at the sleeping form in the buggy.

'She doesn't look very upset now.'

'No. She cried herself to sleep, poor love.'

Nick Hornby

EXTRACTS

Cut along the dotted lines and staple the texts together to make your own handy anthology. Make sure you keep it safe with your Revision Guide.

This extract is from a newspaper article about teenagers and how they earn pocket money.

EXTRACT 5 – WHO'D BE A PAPER BOY?

Who'd be a paper boy?

John Crace
Saturday 11 March 2006

A newspaper round was once a teenager's sole source of pocket money. Not any more, discovers John Crace

It's cold, it's dark and you've got to bolt your breakfast before dragging a bag full of papers round the streets. To add insult to injury, you then have to go to school. So who would be bothered with a paper round? Almost no one these days, it seems.

Twenty years ago, a paper round was one of the few ways for a teenager to earn a few quid to squander on a packet of No 6 and a bottle of cider, and the kids who did it generally took it seriously.

They turned up on time and the right papers were - by and large - delivered to the right houses. Now, a lot of newsagents have given up trying to find kids to do it.

'I stopped deliveries 18 months ago,' says Neesa, who just happens to run Costcutter at the top of my road. 'I had four boys earning £20 a week for delivering about 18 papers each per day, and every day at least one would fail to turn up and I'd have to deliver the papers myself to stop customers getting angry. It was just more trouble than it was worth.'

You can have some sympathy for the kids. Standards in literacy and numeracy have fallen so steeply that it can be a real struggle identifying door names and numbers, and the Sunday papers are now so heavy that your averagely obese teenager just doesn't have the strength or stamina for the job. But the bottom line is that most kids can no longer be bothered to get out of bed for £20.

New research from the Cartoon Network shows that your average kid is raking in £770 a year, of which only £32 comes from paper rounds. Which rather suggests that most teenagers last only about a week and a half in the job before finding it a bit much.

The bulk of the cash comes from pocket money (£186) and part-time work (£256) - selling fags outside the school gates, presumably - but the most telling items are for performance-related pay.

These days, kids extort about £60 a year from their parents for doing household chores and behaving well - both things that used to be just filed under family life.

And if the little darlings can't stretch to a please and thank you, they can always flog a few household items on eBay. Failing that, there's always the tooth fairy. And you thought Tessa Jowell's finances were complicated.

The Guardian

extort, get unfairly   **squander**, waste

Cut along the dotted lines and staple the texts together to make your own handy anthology. Make sure you keep it safe with your Revision Guide.

The extract below is from a speech in Parliament in 1879. The speaker is describing the dreadful conditions in factories that children have to work in and the crippling effects on their health.

EXTRACT 6 – VICTORIAN CHILD LABOUR

The Benefit of the Factory Legislation

The other is the old, the often-repeated, and as often-refuted, argument that the work is light. Light! Why, no doubt, much of it is light, if measured by the endurance of some three or four minutes. But what say you, my Lords, to a continuity of toil, in a standing posture, in a poisonous atmosphere, during 13 hours, with 15 minutes of rest? Why, the stoutest man in England, were he made, in such a condition of things, to do nothing during the whole of that time but be erect on his feet and stick pins in a pincushion, would sink under the burden. What say you, then, of children--children of the tenderest years? Why, they become stunted, crippled, deformed, useless. I speak what I know--I state what I have seen. When I visited Bradford, in Yorkshire, in 1838, being desirous to see the condition of the children--for I knew that they were employed at very early ages in the worsted business....I asked for a collection of cripples and deformities. In a short time more than 80 were gathered in a large courtyard. They were mere samples of the entire mass. I assert without exaggeration that no power of language could describe the varieties, and I may say, the cruelties, in all these degradations of the human form. They stood or squatted before me in all the shapes of the letters of the alphabet. This was the effect of prolonged toil on the tender frames of children at early ages. When I visited Bradford, under the limitation of hours some years afterwards, I called for a similar exhibition of cripples; but, God be praised! there was not one to be found in that vast city. Yet the work of these poor sufferers had been light, if measured by minutes, but terrific when measured by hours.

Hansard's *Parliamentary Debates*. Apr. 4, 1879. 3rd Series, vol. CCXLV, pp. 355-356.

oft-refuted, often contradicted
toil, work
worsted, woollen yarn, or fabric made from that yarn

EXTRACTS

Cut along the dotted lines and staple the texts together to make your own handy anthology. Make sure you keep it safe with your Revision Guide.

This text is from a newspaper article by Ian Beetlestone about London's black taxis, or 'cabs'.

EXTRACT 7 – THE HISTORY OF LONDON'S BLACK CABS

When I picked up my first fare in Covent Garden last month, I couldn't even open the passenger doors. I had two gentlemen fresh from dinner in Langley Street, and I was panicking, pressing all the buttons I could find, fumbling with keys. Nonetheless they were delighted when I told them they were my first, and that consequently the ride – as goes the cabbie tradition – was free, to wherever they wanted to go. Clapham Junction, as it happened, though they might as well have said Tuxedo Junction as far as my frayed nerves were concerned.

When I started learning the Knowledge of London in October 2008, the examiner told us it was the hardest thing we would ever do. He wasn't exaggerating. There are no dropout figures, but each year Transport for London (TfL) usually licenses between a quarter and a third of the number of applicants, so we can safely say that most who start the Knowledge never finish it. The average 'Knowledge Boy' (or, occasionally, Girl) spends three or four years covering around 20,000 miles within a six-mile radius of Charing Cross, out on their moped come rain, freezing wind, or traffic chaos. Hundreds of hours are spent drawing lines on laminated maps of the city, working out the most direct route from hotel to station, restaurant to office, monument to square. We learn thousands of 'points of interest', taking in around 25,000 streets. And we don't just sit an exam, we have a potentially endless series of 'appearances', in which we recite the perfect route between any two points in the city, until the examiners think we're good enough. I had 19 of them over a period of 18 months – many candidates have more.

The terror of the appearance is legendary – ask any cabbie and watch him wince. In the 'olden days', John Mason – head of taxi and private hire at TfL – tells me, the examiners would play games such as putting the chair in the examination room facing the wrong direction, and give an automatic fail to the student who dared turn it around. 'You can't do that in the modern age,' he says. 'I don't think it was acceptable in years gone by, to be frank.' Dean Warrington runs the WizAnn Knowledge school that I attended and got his green badge – the licence that allows drivers to operate across Greater London – in 1996. He remembers one examiner who would choose the start and end points of his questions by throwing two darts into a map, and if the student felt this was unfair he would offer to let them throw the darts instead. 'He was a crazy bloke.' Nowadays the Knowledge seeks to be 'as efficient, fair and transparent as possible,' says Mason. Well, you can't deny the industry needs to modernise.

And it is doing so. You may not have noticed, but the classic cab is being retired. The Austin FX4 was introduced in 1958, updated and rebranded the Fairway in 1987, and is set to all but disappear from the streets of the capital in the new year. Meanwhile, hundreds of its successor – the bubblier TX (drivers often refer to it as the 'Noddy cab') – have been recalled with mechanical problems and, as you may have read, its manufacturer Manganese Bronze has gone into administration. Fairway driver Lionel May tells me, 'You never stop learning', and he turns 80 in January. Will he be sad to hand his Fairway back to the garage? 'Most definitely. It goes like a bomb.' Everybody I speak to about the Fairway raves about its super-reliable engine that can do well over 500,000 miles without any problems.

Not that that's of much concern to the average passenger who only sits in the back for a few minutes at a time. Aesthetics might be though, and it's a gorgeous car. This was a big part of the attraction for some of us Knowledge Boys – not just the car, but the whole beautiful, archaic industry, first licensed by Oliver Cromwell, idiosyncrasies and all. Fellow new driver (we're known as 'butter boys' in the trade, because we take the bread and butter from the mouths of established drivers' families) Andrew Baker eulogises this: 'I've always recognised the job as being something a little bit special, a little bit unusual, a little bit out of the ordinary.' He tells me that when he moved to London to do his degree it was really an excuse to get to the city he'd always wanted to live in, and that it was 'romance' that attracted him to the Knowledge, leaving the degree behind. I too was drawn to it in my mid-30s. In love with London and in a career rut, I saw an opportunity to become a working part of this magical town.

As my old teacher Dean puts it: 'Let's stay the pride of the world's taxi drivers – why not?'

The Guardian December 2012

Cut along the dotted lines and staple the texts together to make your own handy anthology. Make sure you keep it safe with your Revision Guide.

The extract below is from a text published in 1871, in which a Victorian gentleman describes the view from his house in London over a cabstand, and gives his views on the life of the cabmen he watches.

EXTRACT 8 – VICTORIAN CAB DRIVERS

For some little time I have been confined to the house. Instead of going abroad after breakfast, I stay in the dining-room, and I generally manage to limp to the dining-room windows. Now just opposite these windows is a cabstand. I used to think that cabstand a nuisance, but the truth now dawns upon me that there is a compensation in most things.

I am not, I candidly confess, a man of intellectual resources. I rarely look into any books beyond my business book, and, a very little, into a betting-book. The 'Daily Telegraph' kindly manufactures all my opinions for me, and a game of cards is my best enjoyment of an evening. But the D. T. exhausts itself, and I can't very well play at cards in the daylight. So I fall back upon my resources, which frequently resolve themselves into the cabstand.

When I go and look at them after breakfast, it appears to me that the cabman's lot in life is not an unhappy one. His work is not hard; he lives out in the open air; and though he says he has hardly enough to eat, I am quite sure that he gets a little more than is quite good for him to drink. He can go to sleep comfortably on his box, and if it rains he can get inside the carriage. Sometimes the floor of the cab is extemporised into an al fresco [outdoor] dining-table. There is a great deal of horse-play among these fellows. I observe one old man who is in the habit of going contentedly asleep on his box. It is a favourite device for some one to lift up the body of the cab from the ground, shake it, and let it dash upon the earth. One's first notion is that the somnolent driver will have his neck dislocated, or get concussion of the brain, but somehow he seems to hold on. Now this is not all an uncommon type of cabman – a man of extreme animal nature, whose only notion of enjoyment is to drink and sleep in the sunshine. But there are some sharp fellows among them. There is one man who has often a book with him, who has a very sharp pair of spectacles and a distinctive nose of his own, and an expression of countenance which shows him as acute and cynical as any of his betters. I have no doubt but that man has formed opinions of his own on most subjects of human interest, and could maintain them well in an argument. As a rule, the cabmen are content with their newspaper – many of them, indeed, cannot, or do not care to read – and very rarely you see any of them with a book. On the shady side of the street they often seem to enjoy themselves very much, engaging in chaff or talk, reading the newspaper, and every now and then disappearing into a public, to get a penny glass of the vile stuff which they know as London beer. Still business is business, and however grateful may be the charm of leisure, the cabman has a certain sum of money to make up, and he has a quick, alert eye to detect a possible fare in the least roving glance or indecisive movement of a pedestrian.

extemporised, improvised
somnolent, sleepy
chaff, worthless conversation

EXTRACTS

Cut along the dotted lines and staple the texts together to make your own handy anthology. Make sure you keep it safe with your Revision Guide.

Tom Kevill-Davies is passionate about cycling and food. He has cycled all over the world, eating and writing about food. In this extract, he describes arriving in Ecuador, a country in South America.

EXTRACT 9 – THE HUNGRY CYCLIST

After another two days of going uphill I arrived in Ipiales and the border with Ecuador. The air was cold and thin. Gasping for breath I said goodbye to a country I had fallen in love with and entered another. From the border, where the usual money changers, pickpockets and disgruntled border officials did everything to make life worse, I rode towards Quito. But in Ecuador it seemed as though someone had dimmed the lights and turned down the volume. Gone were the smiles and friendly cheers of encouragement from the roadside. Gone were the picturesque colonial farmsteads with their flower-covered porches. Here homes were functional, unfinished concrete, spewing construction steel. It rained, it was cold and I wanted to turn around.

Sheltering from torrential rain in a dirty roadside hamlet just north of Quito, I surveyed my options for dinner. A few limp limbed chickens did another turn in their mechanical rotisserie; a plate of worn-out humitas, a sweet tamale, waited for that unlucky customer to save them from another night under the heat lamp; a bored teenager with too much hair-gel prodded and probed a row of disturbingly red hotdog sausages. Not at all tempted by the usual suspects that made up the options in these small Ecuadorian towns, I began to wonder if my hunger could hold out until breakfast.

But hello! What's this?

At the end of the street, sheltering from the rain under a tatty umbrella, an old lady was fanning frantically at the coals of her small grill. I took a seat on the cold steps of the grocery store from which she served, and watched her work while a steady stream of customers pulled in from the rain.

I ordered a bowl of grilled chicken gizzards, served on a heap of sweet corn and fried kernels of salted maize and it was immediately clear that she knew what she was doing. As the evening passed by the buses, trucks and pick-ups splashed through the rain filled potholes of the main street. We didn't talk much, but that seemed normal here in Ecuador, but from what little was said, and my persistent interest in the secret of her giblets, it was obvious we enjoyed a common love of food, and it wasn't long before our conversation turned to Cuy. I expressed my dismay at having only found this traditional dish strung up like freshly run over roadkill in front of the tourist restaurants en route from Otavalo to Quito, and my keenness to see how these rodents were prepared at home. I was invited for lunch the next day.

Cuy, conejillo de Indias – Indian rabbits, or guinea pigs as we know them in the pet shop – have been an important food source in Peru and Ecuador since pre-Inca times. Fifteen centuries later, they still remain an Andean delicacy, and on average Peruvians and Ecuadorians gobble down twenty two million of these tasty rodents every year. Most Andean households keep cuy at home in the same way that we might keep chickens. Considered a speciality, they are mostly saved for special occasions. Rather like a bottle of champagne or perhaps a box of Ferrero Rocher, a mating pair of guinea pigs are a typical house warming gift for a newlywed couple. Playing an integral role in Andean religious and ceremonial practices, as well as providing dinner, cuy are also used in the traditional medicine of the region. A live cuy is rubbed over the body of someone sick. The cuy's squeaking indicates the diseased area of the human patient.

The Hungry Cyclist by Tom Kevill-Davies

Andean delicacy, a favourite food in the Andes, a mountain range in South America
giblets, liver, heart, gizzard and neck of a chicken or other bird
gizzard, stomach parts
rotisserie, rotating spit for roasting meat

Cut along the dotted lines and staple the texts together to make your own handy anthology. Make sure you keep it safe with your Revision Guide.

A young man writes to his parents from Australia where he has emigrated.

EXTRACT 10 – LETTERS FROM SYDNEY

Sydney, April 9th, 1851

Dear Father and Mother

This comes with my kind love to you both, as also to my brothers and sisters and I hope you will excuse me for not writing before, as I have been so put about. I arrived in Sydney on the 9th of June, after a fine, but long passage, since when I have worked at my trade but two months out of a year and ten months that I have been here. As many others are compelled to do, I was forced to go up the country, 850 miles from Sydney, as a shepherd, at the low wages of £15 per year. If you know of any mechanic who wishes to rusticate at that wage, he will get plenty of that employment here; but if he is inclined to get his living at his trade, he must not come here, but had better stop at home on half a loaf. Tell Jim, it would be no use his coming out here, without he could bring £200 and his tools with him. Then he might barely make as good a living as he makes at home.

I think of working my passage home shortly; but if you do not see me within twelve months from the present date, you may expect to hear from me, either from California or some part of the United States of America, as it is no use my stopping here. I have had some rankles in my lifetime, but this bangs all. It took me just six weeks to travel 850 miles, part of which was a dense forest, 160 miles through, your only companions being kangaroos, emus, cockatoos, parrots etc, with now and then a black fellow and his family to be seen, stark naked, and about every 50 or 70 miles, a lonely shepherd gunya, or bark hut, in which you can lay on your bed, and count every star there is in the heavens. I am very well in health, considering the heat of this part of the world, together with the mosquitos, sand flies, fleas etc, which breed here in millions and constantly annoy you, night and day.

I don't know that I have any more to say at present, than if you write to me, you must write by return of post, and you pay the postage, or I shall not get it, they will not let you pay for a letter here, either going or coming, through which I believe many letters never arrive. This concludes with my kindest love to you all; and I remain

Your affectionate son

Henry Smith

PS Tell Jim to show this letter to Mrs Lambert, and let her know that I am very intimate with Mr Howe; and Mr and Mrs Howe are quite well and all their family, but, like myself, have been sadly knocked about, although, like everybody else, in hopes of doing better. They have not been out of Sydney, but as I have told you before, he has not been half his time in work. They are sadly disappointed at not receiving any letters from home, as he has wrote letters and can get no answer. They often hear from Thomas Lambert and his family, who are all quite well; but, like ourselves, badly employed. Mr Howe will write again very shortly.

Brighton Gazette, 1851

rusticate, go and live in the country

ANSWERS

SECTION A: READING

1. Planning your exam time
A1: 3–4 minutes
A2: 12 minutes

2. Reading texts explained
For example: The facts and figures suggest that the purpose is to inform readers about teenagers' incomes. These statistics also suggest the text is aimed at an adult audience, as adults are likely to be more interested in these research findings. The author's point of view seems to be that modern teenagers are lazy.

3. Reading questions explained 1
The main difference between identifying information (assessment objective 1) and explaining how writers use language (assessment objective 2) is that explaining how writers use language involves looking at how language and structural features are used and what effects they have.

4. Reading questions explained 2
Question A5 (A5 should be circled)

5. Reading the questions
- Both texts
- The whole of each text
- 'compare', 'attitude to children and young people', 'how'
- 12 minutes

6. Skimming for the main idea or theme
For example: Training to be a cab driver in London is hard work but the job is a magical one and one to be proud of.

7. Annotating the texts
Answers could include:
- 'enemy'
- 'grave'
- 'waves rushed in'
- 'out into the darkness'.

8. Putting it into practice
Answers should identify at least two further points, for example:
- The narrator is capable of keeping calm and methodical under pressure, as he 'grabbed' the bolt and (he said) 'filled my lungs with air'.
- He has a fighting spirit, as he is 'determined to hang on', and also has the self-control to wait for the best moment to let go.

9. Putting it into practice
Answers should identify at least three further points, for example:
- The observation that 'There is a great deal of horse-play' suggests the writer thinks that life as a cab driver is fun and free of responsibility.
- The words 'going contentedly asleep' suggest not only that there is time in a cab driver's day to sleep during working hours but also that the driver has no worries; he is content with his life.
- The writer's comment that you 'very rarely see any of them with a book' highlights his idea that the cab drivers are uneducated.

10. Explicit information and ideas
1 20 years ago
2 £770
3 Cartoon Network

11. Implicit ideas
Answers should include four points, for example:
- He bought comics that suited the children's individual interests.
- He didn't take them to places where they would be barred or out of place.
- He even made 'no-man's land' seem attractive with a picnic.
- He introduced them to nature.

12. Inference
Answers should include and explain four short quotations, for example:
- 'gaped' suggests Manderley is wide open and looks vacant or deserted
- 'barrier' suggests narrator is being prevented from entering
- 'long, tenacious fingers' and 'triumphed' show that nature keeps reaching out and is taking control
- 'white, naked limbs' creates frightening, ghost-like image of the trees.

Answers should also include a summary of the whole point, for example:
- Manderley is presented as an eerie place, abandoned to nature.

13. Interpreting information and ideas
A man who could read and write and was well educated.

14. Point – Evidence – Explanation
For example: Quotation – 'dragging a bag'; Explanation – 'This suggests that a paper round is hard, physical work, where the load is so heavy it can only be dragged, not carried.'

15. Putting it into practice
Answers should identify and explain three further points, for example:
- The narrator keeps trying even though he describes the ship as a 'grave'.
- The narrator waits and plans despite being tired and frightened.
- Even though he 'choked on soot', the narrator still carries on.

16. Putting it into practice
Answers should identify and explain three further points, for example:
- Only 'between a quarter and a third' of applicants are licensed, showing how difficult it is to succeed.
- Applicants need to do around 20,000 miles of practice, emphasising the hard work involved.
- The writer did not have just one exam but 19 'appearances' in front of examiners, highlighting the rigorous nature of the assessment.

17. Word classes
Answers should consist of two sentences and include comments on the use of, for example:
- Nouns to create the picture of the ship (e.g. 'stern', 'rail', 'deck').
- Verbs to highlight the actions of the narrator (e.g. 'Clinging', 'waved', 'grabbed').
- Verbs to show the panic of the musicians (e.g. 'scrambled', 'scraping').

18. Connotations
For example:
- 'endurance' literally means something that lasts; here, it has connotations of a never-ending amount of time putting up with something hard and dangerous

- 'poisonous' literally means toxic; here, it has connotations of death, as though the air in the factory could literally kill the children
- 'burden' literally means heavy load; here, the connotation is that the children are weighed down and exhausted by the work.

19. Figurative language

Answers should identify and explain the effect of at least two examples of figurative language, for example:

- 'gaped' – the personification of window suggests the narrator is being stared at from within the house
- 'like the archway of a church' – this simile suggests the narrator is entering somewhere sacred.

20. Creation of character

Answers should use a P-E-E structure and should identify and explain two examples of how dialogue is used to create character, for example:

- Point – Will is presented as having little patience with children; Evidence – 'Just leave it. What's the problem?'; Explanation – suggests Will is irritated and uninterested.
- Point – Marcus is presented as nervous and under-confident; Evidence – 'I don't know. Maybe. Maybe…'; Explanation – suggests Marcus doesn't want to tell the truth, perhaps because he's worried about the reaction.

21. Creating atmosphere

Answers could include:

- 'gone native now' – the personification of the shrubs suggests danger and gives the impression of an impenetrable jungle
- 'rearing' – a verb with connotations of animal strength
- 'monster height' – an adjective suggesting danger or threat
- 'parasites' – a noun carrying negative connotations of infection and disease.

Answers should also include an overview of the overall mood or tone, for example:

- The overall tone is a menacing one, where nature is threatening and dangerous.

22. Narrative voice

For example:

The third-person omniscient narration allows the reader to 'hear' Marcus's thoughts. For example, the writer describes how Marcus begins to justify what he has done by calling the duck 'pathetic' and suggesting that the death was 'just a coincidence'. This reveals to the reader that Marcus is worried and perhaps a little frightened about what will happen to him next.

(Note that effective P-E-E paragraphs should use connecting phrases to link and develop the point.)

23. Putting it into practice

Answers should identify and explain three further points, for example:

- The connotations of 'church' are of somewhere sacred, quiet and still, which add to the tension of the passage.
- The metaphor 'strange embrace' describing the tangle of branches suggests something uncomfortable and out of place.
- The verbs 'crowded' and 'leant' describe nature as threatening and suggest danger.

24. Putting it into practice

For example:

These phrases contrast with the 'pleasure-grounds' mentioned in the rhetorical question and suggest that **the narrator has mixed feelings about his childhood**.

Answers should also make two further points, including reference to the first-person narrative voices, for example:

- The use of first-person narration creates the idea that the family was a tight unit, through repeated use of 'we' and 'our'.
- The childhood is described as a time of safety, with the parents creating a safe family in the 'warmth of their arms'.

25. Rhetorical devices 1

Answers could include:

- The alliteration in 'insult to injury' reinforces the sarcastic suggestion that a paper round is hard work.
- The colloquial language of 'kids' and 'fags' helps to build up the idea that the writer looks down on teenagers today as lazy.

26. Rhetorical devices 2

Answers should identify and explain two examples of rhetorical devices, for example:

- The personification 'worn-out' used to describe the unappetising food on offer is used to elicit the reader's sympathy for the hungry narrator.
- The hyperbole of the phrase 'save them from another night under the heat lamp' adds humour but also a growing sense for the reader of how hard it is for the narrator to find something good to eat.

27. Fact, opinion and expert evidence

Fact: 'kids extort about £60 a year from their parents'.
Opinion: 'Which rather suggests that most teenagers last only about a week and a half in the job before finding it a bit much.'
Expert evidence: "I had four boys earning £20 a week for delivering about 18 papers each per day, and every day at least one would fail to turn up…"

28. Identifying sentence types

1 Multi-clause (subordinate)
2 Single-clause
3 Multi-clause (coordinate)
4 Minor

29. Commenting on sentence types

For example:

Two short sentences are used at the end of the extract that suggest tension is coming in the narrative. The first short sentence sums up the happiness expressed earlier in the paragraph but is then followed by another short sentence that changes the mood as it starts with the word 'but'.

30. Structure: non-fiction

Answers could include the following points:

- Letter starts and ends with only a brief mention of love but is full of details of hardships the writer has endured, which might suggest the writer is finding his experience difficult.
- The writer uses a long middle paragraph to give details of his hard journey, suggesting his focus is on the difficulties he has faced.
- The writer uses a postscript to give news about other people; as the detail here also focuses on hardships, it suggests the writer is aware that he is not alone in the difficulties he has faced.

31. Structure: fiction

Answers could identify:

- Use of closely described action, presented in list form, reinforces the sense of danger and tension.
- Repetition of pronoun 'I' reflects the focus on the narrator's own battle for survival.
- Continued use of repetition ('down, down' and 'waited, waited') adds to the tension and suspense.
- Paragraph ends on a positive note ('with all my strength'), suggesting the narrator's determination to survive.

32. Putting it into practice

Answers could include:

- The use of a three-sentence paragraph, with sentences starting long and getting shorter to end with the cliffhanger 'This was it', builds tension.
- The combination of dialogue with Marcus's thoughts creates both humour and tension as the writer reveals to the reader Marcus's reaction to the adults' anger.
- The detailed dialogue suggests a real conversation, which increases tension as the reader experiences the scene in full.

33. Putting it into practice

Answers could include:

- The writer starts a paragraph suggesting he has 'some sympathy for the kids', but then follows this short sentence with sarcasm about their lack of stamina, suggesting a negative opinion of modern teenagers.
- The repetition of the colloquial language 'kid' suggests a lack of respect for teenagers.
- The facts and statistics from the Cartoon Network, an expert source, makes the writer's argument believable and trustworthy.
- The emotive language 'extort' makes the teenagers sound almost criminal, reinforces the writer's negative opinion of them.
- The use of the sarcastic 'little darlings' at the end confirms the writer's view.

34. Handling two texts

1 Question A6 (the comparison question), which is worth 10 marks.
2 Two or three (note you should also take an overview).
3 Question A6 (the comparison question).

35. Selecting evidence for synthesis

For example:
The weather is bad in both texts: in *The Hungry Cyclist* the rain is 'torrential' and in *Letters from Sydney* the heat causes hardship.

36. Synthesising evidence

For example:
Both writers found the weather to be a big problem. In Ecuador, the writer had to shelter from the 'torrential rain', and in Sydney the writer of the letter suffered due to the insects brought out by the heat.

37. Looking closely at language

Answers should identify and explain two further points, for example:

- The figures and statistics '20,000' and '25,000' are used to emphasise the difficulty faced.
- The pattern of three 'rain, freezing wind, or traffic chaos' also emphasises the challenge involved in the training.
- Long sentences containing lists of information show how intense the training is by building up the sense of all the requirements.
- The paragraph ends with 'many candidates have more' after a hyphen, which emphasises how rigorous the assessment is.

38. Planning to compare

For example:
Both writers use a pattern of three to engage their audience. However, in *Who'd Be a Paper Boy?*, this device is used to set the light-hearted tone, with the alliteration in 'bolt your breakfast' helping to reinforce the sarcasm, whereas in *Victorian Child Labour* the writer uses it for emphasis. Here, the repetition of the word 'light' is used together with the pattern of three to get across the message that the labour is hard.

39. Comparing ideas

Answers should include two pieces of evidence, one from each text. For example:
Crace uses sarcasm ('identifying door names' is a 'real struggle') to describe what the paper round involves, whereas Hansard uses emotive language ('toil', 'poisonous', 'cripple') to reinforce the factory work.

40. Comparing perspective

For example:
In *The History of London's Black Cabs*, the writer maintains the perspective that driving a cab in London is difficult, but he also introduces more positive elements about the 'whole beautiful, archaic industry'. On the other hand, the perspective in *Victorian Cab Drivers* remains much the same throughout – that the life of a cab driver is a pleasant one.

41. Answering a compare question

For example:
Both texts are about children working, but *Who'd Be a Paper Boy?* aims to highlight the laziness of modern teenagers, while *Victorian Child Labour* emphasises the harsh conditions of factory work in the 1800s. Both texts use a pattern of three to engage their audience and present their ideas. In *Who'd Be a Paper Boy?* Crace uses 'It's cold, it's dark and you've got to bolt your breakfast' to emphasise the unattractive aspects of a paper round. Similarly, Hansard uses a pattern of three in 'the old, the often-repeated, and as often-refuted, argument' to stress his perspective, although here the tone and message are more serious.

42. Putting it into practice

Answers could include:

- In *Victorian Cab Drivers*, the writer appears to criticise drivers with the use of emotive terms like 'extreme animal nature', whereas in *The History of London's Black Cabs*, the perspective is that drivers train hard and should be respected and a paragraph is used to give extensive details of the training.
- Both texts use lists: *Victorian Cab Drivers* uses a list of three including 'his work is not hard' to suggest cab drivers have an easy life, while lists are used in *The History of London's Black Cabs* to emphasise how difficult the job is, giving details of how they spend the 'Hundreds of hours' of training.
- In *Victorian Cab Drivers*, long sentences are used to create a serious tone and emphasise the writer's negative attitude towards the cab drivers, whereas *The History of London's Black Cabs* uses a variety of sentence structures. The shorter sentence at the end of the second paragraph in *The History of London's Black Cabs* highlights how hard it is to become qualified.
- The perspective in *The History of London's Black Cabs* is personal, as the writer has worked as a cab driver and understands the 'terror of the appearance' that they face in order to qualify. The writer of *Victorian Cab Drivers*, on the other hand, simply observes the cab drivers from the comfort of his home.

43. Evaluating a text: fiction

Answers should include two inferences, for example:

- Despite the restrictions, the father made an effort to find enjoyable things they were allowed to do.
- The father provided treats for the children, such as dancing lessons and chess.
- He chose comics that suited their interests.
- The father is presented as interested in his children's education: he played chess with the narrator and chose 'publications from England' that were more challenging than 'supermen' comics.

44. Evaluating a text: non-fiction

Answers should include two points, for example:

- The writer feels he has faced far worse than the 'rankles' he has faced in the past and feels that the journey was one of extreme hardship.
- Despite the hardship the writer is still 'very well in health', and in his postscript he mentions other people who are 'quite well'; this suggests that his overall view is too pessimistic. There must be something good about Australia if they are all still healthy.
- Overall, the writer stresses the lack of suitable work and ends the postscript on this point, which suggests he did have unrealistic ideas about life in Australia and is a bit resentful.

45. Using evidence to evaluate

Answers should include two P-E-E paragraphs, for example:

- Point – The writer is not happy about his experience in Australia; Evidence – he says he has been 'so put about'; Explanation – this suggests he feels he has had to face one problem after another.
- Point – The writer feels trapped; Evidence – use of words 'compelled' and 'forced'; Explanation – this suggests he has no control over his situation and that there is no alternative for him.

(Note that answers should use a clear P-E-E structure with very short quotations or paraphrasing.)

46. Putting it into practice

For example:

- Marcus is worried about what the adults will think, which may make a reader sympathetic towards him.
- Marcus jokes about the dead duck, which suggests he is not very caring about animals.
- Marcus is shown to be a pessimist, as the passage ends with him convinced he will be found guilty. This may lose a reader's sympathy, as he is presented as very negative.

47. Putting it into practice

Answers could include:

- Challenging at the start – Hansard questions his audience to gain their attention and make them listen closely. This is important as it is a speech and suggests Hansard feels strongly about his topic.
- Hansard has personal experience of the topic he is discussing – 'I state what I have seen'. This makes his points more persuasive and powerful.
- Hansard uses specific evidence about his visit and goes into detail about the effects of child labour. This makes his speech seem truthful.
- The writer creates a vivid picture of the effects of child labour, which is very powerful and might have shocked the audience.

SECTION B: WRITING

48. Writing questions: an overview

- Component 2 – transactional/persuasive writing
- Two
- One

49. Writing questions: Component 1

Answers should include at least 5 or 6 ideas.

50. Writing questions: Component 2

Answers should include at least 5 or 6 ideas for each of the two questions, for example:

B1 – helping the elderly, working in a charity shop, mentoring younger students; meet people with different backgrounds and experiences, feels good to help others, enriching; report – formal language, paragraphs, introduction, recommendation, conclusion

B2 (arguing against) – students and teachers alike need a longer break over the summer to rest and recharge, the temperatures in July and August are not optimal for learning or concentration, two weeks is not long enough to go for a proper holiday abroad, while two weeks might be easier for working parents, a longer break offers students better opportunities to get work experience or get involved in volunteering; letter – name and address of recipient, Dear…, subject line, Yours faithfully/sincerely

51. Writing for a purpose: creative

For example: The rays of warm sunshine raced across the room as I flung back the curtains. Thoughts of the day to come danced through my mind as my eager eyes searched the street for signs of his arrival. I fidgeted impatiently. The syrupy tower of pancakes, the lake of fizzy drink and the mountain of cake were now just hours from my lips. (Senses: 'warm' (touch), 'searched' (sight) 'syrupy' (taste).)

Verbs to show not tell: 'flung', 'danced', 'fidgeted'. Figurative language: 'sunshine raced' (personification); 'tower of pancakes, the lake of fizzy drink and the mountain of cake' (metaphors).

52. Writing for a purpose: inform, explain, review

1 For example: Finding their feet; A typical day; New subjects; What's on the menu?; Extra-curricular activities.

2 For example: I would use an informal tone to appear friendly and supportive, but with standard English to reflect the adult audience.

3 For example: research suggests the majority of students settle in by the end of the autumn term; surveys show 50% of Year 7s have suffered from anxiety at some point in their first term.

53. Writing for a purpose: argue and persuade

1 For example: Sports facilities are vital in the fight against obesity; young people need to be encouraged to take up sports; there are enough cinemas already in the town.

2 For example: Yes, a cinema will encourage the opening of new restaurants in the area, but these will have an impact on existing food outlets that will lose business.

3 For example: Do we really need to give local people any more excuses to sit on their ever-widening backsides? [Hyperbole ('ever-widening backsides'), rhetorical question]; You must surely agree that closing the sports centre can only add to the lazy lethargy that already looms too large in our town. [Direct address ('you'), alliteration ('lazy lethargy…looms too large')]; The big screen, the fizzy drinks and the bottomless bucket of popcorn may sound appealing but are not as good for us as fresh air and exercise [Pattern of three ('big screen, the fizzy drinks and the bottomless bucket'), alliteration ('bottomless bucket')]

54. Writing for an audience
For example: You may think you've got ages to prepare for your GCSEs. You may think you don't need to worry about them just yet. But time flies and it won't be long before you're sitting in that exam hall. So it's important to start getting ready for them now. (Note the use of some informal features, e.g. abbreviations such as 'you've', which are appropriate to this audience but would not be in a more formal text.)

55. Putting it into practice
For example:
Timing plan – 45 minutes total: 10 mins planning; 30 mins writing; 5 mins checking
Notes on title options – (a) and (c) could draw on personal experience; (b) quite open; (d) has to be a narrative
Decision – My Favourite Room.
Narrative voice I will use – first person; Ideas for language techniques – five senses, metaphors for objects/furniture.

56. Putting it into practice
Spider diagrams with ideas, for example:
B1 – Audience, teenage (Year 11 assembly); Purpose, persuade; Topic, joining the youth club; Form, speech
B2 – Audience, general public (possibly other teenagers/young people); Purpose, inform/persuade; Topic, favourite holiday destination; Form, article for website

57. Form: articles and reviews
Answers could include:
1 Reviews use figurative language, articles are more formal
2 Reviews contain writer's opinions; articles use quotations from other people as evidence
3 Articles are intended to be factual and trustworthy, whereas reviews are more emotive and personal.

58. Form: letters and reports
1 Letter
2 Report
3 Letter (could be informal)

59. Form: information guides
For example:
Heading – Golden Rules for Good Behaviour
Sub-headings – Top rules (list), What to wear (paragraphs, possibly a list), Moving around the school (paragraphs), Rules about food (paragraphs), Rules to remember (conclusion, paragraph)

60. Putting it into practice
For example:
Headline – Teenagers of Today: Rebels or Role Models
Sub-heading – A local teenager reveals the truth about our young people
Short opening paragraph – It has recently been claimed that the teenagers in our community are agents of trouble, intent on bad behaviour and making a nuisance of themselves. It is a picture many of us are willing to believe, yet does it paint the whole truth?
Developed paragraph – There are of course those who think it does. However, at the end of my road, in a small, unassuming house, lives a young person who defies this image of dangerous delinquent on a daily basis. Jemima Johnson acts not for recognition or for praise, or because she was asked to help. Jemima acts because she has noticed someone in need and has understood that she can make a difference. What does she do? Every day, Jemima accompanies her elderly neighbour to the local shop, providing Mrs Forbes with an arm to lean on, the chance for a little daily exercise and a hand with the groceries. Of Jemima, Mrs Forbes says, 'She is an angel. I don't know what I'd do without her'. And Jemima is not alone.

61. Ideas and planning: creative
Plans should include four or five key ideas and a range of supporting details, including appropriate language techniques.

62. Structure: creative
Plans should use the five-part narrative structure and include supporting details about language techniques.

63. Beginnings and endings: creative
For example:
Opening 1 (vivid description) – The house sat still and silent, squatting low as if to keep out winter's stinging embrace as the dark night pressed forward, its penetrating stare painting the windows black as coal. Inside...
Opening 2 (dialogue) – 'What was that?' squeaked Adam, his eyes wide with fright, his brow furrowed.
'I don't know,' breathed Henry, the quivering syllables leaving his lips in a whisper...
Opening 3 (mystery) – I know now that it was a mistake. A big one. I should have left things as they were – peaceful, familiar, safe. And yet, that evening...
Opening 4 (conflict or danger) – A whining creak. A floorboard. Where were they? I could see nothing in the pitch and edged around the doorframe into the hall...
Ending (to Opening 1) – I was glad, then, and after all that had passed, to be cradled as I was in the peaceful dark. The night was now familiar to me, its hold as comforting as the arms of an old friend. As I stretched out my tired limbs and pulled the blanket closer to me, I closed my eyes, my lips falling into a sleepy smile. It was good to be home.

64. Putting it into practice
For example:
Ending plan – link back to title; opening the door causes lifelong mystery as narrator never finds out what is in the package, after years of suspense and worry, owner turns up on doorstep and takes it away; use figurative language, metaphor to describe.
First two paragraphs of the answer should follow the plan on page 64 and use one or more of the techniques from page 63.

65. Ideas and planning: inform, explain, review
For example:
Introduction:
- Give overview of situation – that there is not enough to do, youth club will have many benefits

Key point – Current situation
- Firstly...young people have little to do
- They can get in trouble.

Key point – Activities
- List of sports, clubs, etc.
- Include something for both boys and girls.

Key point – Benefits
- Fitness – use expert opinion
- Less trouble in school
- Could do homework in club – use rhetorical question
- Charity events – use emotive language.

Conclusion – Finally...
- Suggest that students could decorate club to save money.

66. Ideas and planning: argue and persuade
A possible plan:
- Introduction – hundreds of channels, 24 hours a day, television can dominate.
- Point 1 – TV can be informative/educational.
- Point 2 – shared experience of high quality drama, etc. (no different to theatre but cheaper and more accessible).
- Counter-argument: some say it takes over our lives; they need to learn how to turn it off.
- Conclusion: like anything, TV is good and bad; it depends on how it's used. Used carefully/selectively it can bring people together, entertain, inform and educate.

67. Openings: transactional/persuasive

1 For example

- Are you one of those who views skateboarding as a teenage hobby rather than a 'real sport'? Think again.
- 85% of teenagers fail to take the recommended amount of exercise each day. 30% are obese by the age of 15. A skateboard ramp is therefore not an expensive luxury – it is a necessity.
- When I was seven, my parents bought me my first skateboard. It wasn't very expensive; they thought it would just be a weekend wonder. Now I'm the British under-21 champion.

2 For example:

- 85% of teenagers fail to take the recommended amount of exercise each day. 30% are obese by the age of 15. A skateboard ramp is therefore not an expensive luxury – it is a necessity.
- As a nation, we must do something about the appalling state of our teenagers' health. Too many young people are too inactive, they spend hours every day surfing the internet, playing computer games and posting pictures on social media sites. They catch the bus for every short journey, use the lift rather than the stairs and remain motionless all evening in front of a screen. A skateboard ramp could change all that.
- (Note that the bold statistical opening has been left as one paragraph to shock the reader. The next paragraph develops the argument set out in the introduction, using appropriate techniques: emotive language ('appalling'), repetition ('they') and patterns of three.)

68. Conclusions: transactional/persuasive

For example:
A skateboard ramp is neither an expensive luxury nor an unacceptable eye sore, but rather a vital step in encouraging our young people to move away from a static world of immobility and towards a happier, healthier and more active future. Skateboarding may not appeal to everyone, but for some it could make all the difference, helping them to feel fitter and more fulfilled. And isn't a happy, healthy and active life what we want for our young people?
(Note the first sentence of this conclusion summarises the writer's argument; the second adds a positive note; the final sentence asks a rhetorical question, further promoting the argument.)

69. Putting it into practice

Effective plans will include:

- ideas for an introduction and conclusion
- a range of key points
- some developed detail for each key point
- key points logically sequenced.

70. Paragraphing for effect

If students choose to add a paragraph to the first example they should use Point-Evidence-Explain.
If they have added a paragraph to the second example they need to have clearly introduced the reader to the content of the paragraph then developed it and added detail.

71. Linking ideas

For example:
This morning, my sister proved that she is the most annoying person on earth. **Firstly**, she finished all the milk so there was none left for me. **Then** she spent an hour in the bathroom. **Finally**, she borrowed my headphones without asking and wouldn't give them back.
On the other hand, she can be thoughtful. **For example**, she made me a delicious lasagne the other day. **Similarly**, she always remembers my birthday and buys me great presents.

72. Putting it into practice

Effective answers will:

- be structured using Point-Evidence-Explain
- sequence and signal their argument using a range of adverbials.

73. Vocabulary for effect: synonyms

For example: The idea of celebrities as perfect role models is not the only misguided ~~idea~~ concept connected with the world of the ~~celebrity~~ famous. Some people have the ~~idea~~ notion that ~~celebrities~~ superstars should be consulted on everything from international politics to haircare.

74. Vocabulary for effect: argue and persuade

For example: In the UK at this very moment hundreds of children, some as young as five, are being kept in appalling conditions. They are caged for up to seven hours a day. They are often made to sit in silence while aggressive adults hurl abuse at them. They are subjected to a ruthless regime of punishments. Most shockingly of all, this brutal and barbaric treatment is accepted as normal despite the suffering it causes.
Note:

- the use of negative emotive language (appalling, ruthless, etc.) to emphasise the paragraph's central idea
- language chosen for its connotations of imprisonment and torture (caged, brutal, barbaric).

75. Language for different effects 1

For example:

- rhetorical question – Do you want to live a long and healthy life?
- contrast – Roaming the great outdoors and breathing lungfuls of fresh air in the sunshine are much more enjoyable than sitting in a stale, airless room staring mindlessly at the television
- list – Obesity can increase your risk of diabetes, heart attack, depression, arthritis, liver failure and breathing difficulties
- repetition – Exercise can improve your health. Exercise can improve your happiness. Exercise can change your life.

76. Language for different effects 2

For example:

- direct address – You would never believe the pressure my mum inflicted on me
- pattern of three – She nagged, pestered and hounded me for days
- hyperbole – I thought my head was going to explode
- alliteration – This was going to be the most miserable minute of my entire life.

77. Language for different effects 3

For example:

- simile – For many young people, childhood is **like a race** which should be won as soon as possible
- metaphor – Childhood **is a rare and precious jewel** which we should treasure
- personification – This relentless pressure **batters children** and their childhood into the ground.

78. Using the senses

For example:

- Bed – touch – so many crumbs it feels like the seaside, memory of eating biscuits at midnight.
- Under bed – smell leads nose to under bed, touch – furry shapes turn out to be smelly socks, personify into small animals, huddling together for warmth in burrow made of human hair.
- Chest of drawers – sight – armies of empty deodorant cans. Casualties of war. Use taste to identify contents of rows of glasses.

79. Narrative voice

Answers could include:
First-person advantages – allows reader to identify with narrator, creates tension as not all events are known by reader.
First-person disadvantages – limits the narrative events, gives limited information about other characters' feelings and motives.
Third-person advantages – allows reader to know everything, can show feelings/thoughts of any character.
Third-person disadvantages – lacks personal feel created by first-person narrative.

80. Putting it into practice

Effective answers should include:
- a wide and varied vocabulary
- simile, metaphor and personification used sparingly
- some use of appropriate techniques, such as alliteration, facts, opinions.

Your letter should argue and counter-argue the benefits and possible dangers of owning a dog. Remember to use adverbials to link your key points and paragraphs.

81. Putting it into practice

Effective answers should include:
- a wide and varied vocabulary
- simile, metaphor and personification used sparingly
- some description using the senses.

82. Sentence variety 1

For example:
- single-clause – My bedroom is tiny.
- multi-clause sentence (subordinate clause) – If the window ever got cleaned, I would have a lovely view.
- multi-clause sentence (coordinate clause) – The carpet is old and the curtains are threadbare.
- multi-clause sentence (relative clause) – The window, which is about the size of a postage stamp, is filthy.
- minor – Lovely.

83. Sentence variety 2

For example:
- pronoun – I was waiting alone in a classroom.
- article – An eerie silence had fallen.
- preposition – Beyond the classroom door, I heard footsteps.
- *-ing* word – Holding my breath, I waited.
- adjective – Empty and cold, the classroom did nothing to comfort me.
- adverb – Slowly I realised there was a man standing in the doorway.
- conjunction – Although I had never seen him before, I knew immediately why he was there.

84. Sentences for different effects

For example:
- In order to encourage as many students as possible to participate, it will be vital to offer a wide and varied range of sports and sports-related activities, from yoga and dance to gymnastics and cross-country running. Football and netball will not suffice.

(Note that the first sentence has been intentionally extended using multiple clauses.)
- However wide the range of sports you offer, and however flexible the activity schedule may be, these things will not be enough to attract students without a highly effective publicity campaign.

(Note how the key information is placed in the final clause.)

85. Putting it into practice

Effective answers should:
- use a range of sentence types
- use a range of sentence lengths
- start sentences in a variety of ways
- feature sentences structured for effect.

86. Ending a sentence

For example:
I was born in the countryside **and** I grew up surrounded by the sounds and smells of the natural world. When I was ten we moved to the city. **It** was a confusing, fast-paced, deafening environment that I found hard to love. It was such a big change – **and** it came as quite a shock to my system. **W**orst of all I had to leave all my friends behind and try to make new ones in this strange, unfamiliar place. I was lonely **and** convinced I would never feel at home **but** before a year had passed I had the best friend anyone could wish for.

87. Commas

For example:
A list – A bottle of water, an apple, a cereal bar, a torch and a sticking plaster are all things my mother insists I take with me on every school trip.
Main + subordinate clause – Although some school trips take us to places that don't interest me, I always learn something new and interesting.
Main + relative clause – The coach journeys, which invariably make me travel sick and seem to last for hours, are my least favourite part of each trip.

88. Apostrophes and speech punctuation

The corrections are shown in bold.
'There**'**s nothing I can do**,**' said Gary**'**s dad.
'**A**re you sure**?**' replied Gary.
'**I** don**'**t know what you mean**,**' **s**aid his dad.
'**I** think you do**.**'

89. Colons, semi-colons, dashes, brackets and ellipses

1 A colon.
2 A semi-colon.
3 To add, mid-sentence, information which is extra but not entirely necessary.

90. Putting it into practice

Effective answers should include a range of accurate punctuation including commas, apostrophes, colons and semi-colons.

91. Common spelling errors 1

Are students spotting all their spelling mistakes?

92. Common spelling errors 2

The corrections are shown in bold.
I saw Annabel walk **past** wearing **your** shoes. She was carrying **your** bag **too**. I don't know **whose** coat she had on but it had **two** stripes across the back. She stopped and took it **off**. I don't know **where** she was going or what she was up **to**. It was very strange.

93. Common spelling errors 3

Are students using effective strategies to learn words?

94. Proofreading

Are students spotting errors in their writing?

95. Putting it into practice

Effective answers should contain at least five corrected mistakes.

For your own notes

For your own notes

For your own notes

For your own notes

For your own notes

Published by Pearson Education Limited, 80 Strand, London, WC2R 0RL.

www.pearsonschoolsandfecolleges.co.uk

Typeset by Tech-Set Ltd, Gateshead
Produced by Out of House Publishing

Illustrated by Tech-Set Ltd, Gateshead
Cover illustration by Miriam Sturdee

First published 2015

18 17
10 9 8 7 6 5 4 3

British Library Cataloguing in Publication Data
A catalogue record for this book is available from the British Library

ISBN 9781447988106

Printed in Slovakia by Neografia

Acknowledgements

We are grateful to the following for permission to reproduce copyright material:

Extract 1. from *Rebecca*, Curtis Brown (du Maurier D 1938), Reproduced with permission of Curtis Brown Group Ltd, London, on behalf of The Chichester Partnership, Copyright © The Estate of Daphne Du Maurier 1938; Extract 2, from *Every Man for Himself*, Johnson and Alcock and Little, Brown Book Group (UK) (Bainbridge, B 1996); Extract 3. from *My Son's Story*, A P Watt at United Agents LLP (Gordimer N 1990) A P Watt at United Agents LLP, United Agents LLP on behalf of Felix Licensing BV; Extract 4. from *About a Boy*, Penguin (Hornby N 1998), From ABOUT A BOY by Nick Hornby, copyright © 1998 by Nick Hornby. Used by permission of Riverhead, an imprint of Penguin Publishing Group, a division of Penguin Random House LLC; Extract 5. from Who'd be a paper boy?, *The Guardian*, 11/03/2006 (Crace J) The Guardian; Extract 7. from The history of London's black cabs, *The Guardian*, 09/12/2012 (Beetlestone I) The Guardian; Extract 9. from *The Hungry Cyclist*, Harper Collins (Kevill-Davies T 2009) Harper Collins; Extract on page 57. from Transformers: Age of Extinction, review: 'spectacular junk', *The Telegraph*, 25/03/15 (Collin R) Telegraph, copyright © Telegraph Media Group Limited; Extract on page 57. from The truth about lying: it's the hands that betray you, not the eyes, *The Independent*, 12/07/2012 (Sherwin, A.)